MW00603687
Genete Iyesus
Kidus Giyorgis
Omedla Str.
CHIROMEDA
WO 01
Hamle 19 Public
Cure International
Ethiopian's Meeting center
WO 02
Sheihk Jewhar Shonke
Abo
ANKORCHA
Miskayehizuona Medhane Alem
Netsa Art village
Mulu Wengel
Ferensay
SIDEST KILO
Tsahafi Tiezaz Afework Str.
WO 03
Lideta Maryam
Angola Str.
G.Mulugeta Bulli Str.
AABE
Sq. Marx
German Church
JANMEDA
ETCC
WO 04
Defence Force Referal
BELA
YEKA
Washa Mikael And Ankorcha Teklehaymanot
MIST KILO
Russia Str.
Menelik II
Addis MC
Catholic Kidane Mihiret
WO 07
ARAT KILO
KEBENA
Qu.Elisabeth Str.
AAU Sc.Faculty
Kidus Mathews Anglican
Green Valley
Ras Amba
Gymnasium
Kebena Medhane Alem
Comoros Str.
Menbere Tsehaot Kidist Selassie
Adis View
Bel Air
Bale Weld
Dejazmach Wolde Gebriel Str.
Lorenzo Taezaz Str.
Fikre Maryam Aba Techan Str.
Balderas
Cot D'ivoire Str.
Yeka Debre Sahl Kidus Mikael
FITE BER
WO 08
Wele
SIGNAL

Addis Ababa

the new flower of Africa

Edited by: Myrna L. Smith

infoAddis Publishing, LLC
P.O. Box 10819
Alexandria, VA 22310
www.infoAddis.com

ISBN: 978-0-9856829-1-0

Front Cover: Yellow daisy flowers blossom abundantly in Addis Ababa during the month of September/Meskerem, the first month in the Ethiopian calendar. The image of the flower is used in this book as a symbolic representation of the city's past history, current charm, and future potential. Dust jacket front leaf: A photo of the painting of Empress Taitu located in the Addis Ababa Museum

AUTHOR'S NOTE

Why do I write books about Ethiopia? I thought my reason was to tell people about my amazing experience of this extraordinary landscape, culture, history and people. However, as I evaluate my life, I conclude that every experience was preparing me for this one.

I was born and raised in Addis Ababa, Ethiopia. When I went abroad, my experience and knowledge of my homeland could only be described as embryonic. Therefore, learning about myself was a commitment I intended to satisfy, and learning about Ethiopia was the stepping-stone to get me there. This is my birth country, and these are the people from whom I inherited part of my identity.

I traveled throughout Ethiopia, and I noticed that, in addition to their diverse culture and rich history, the people of Ethiopia unite through their own long-held, common values. In accomplishment, their humility shines; in hospitality, their generosity extends to self-sacrifice. What I found was an innate beauty and quality in the simplicity of their lives.

Without making the effort to connect to what was, we limit our understanding of what is. My study of Ethiopia, Africa's oldest independent country, rewarded me with a deep appreciation of the country's culture and rich history. It informed me about events I had once dismissed as irrelevant, by exposing me to new ways of looking at the human spirit. The experience permanently changed my outlook on life to one more inclusive.

So, why do I write books about Ethiopia? I have to! ... to tell you about my people and inspire you to visit them.

Contents

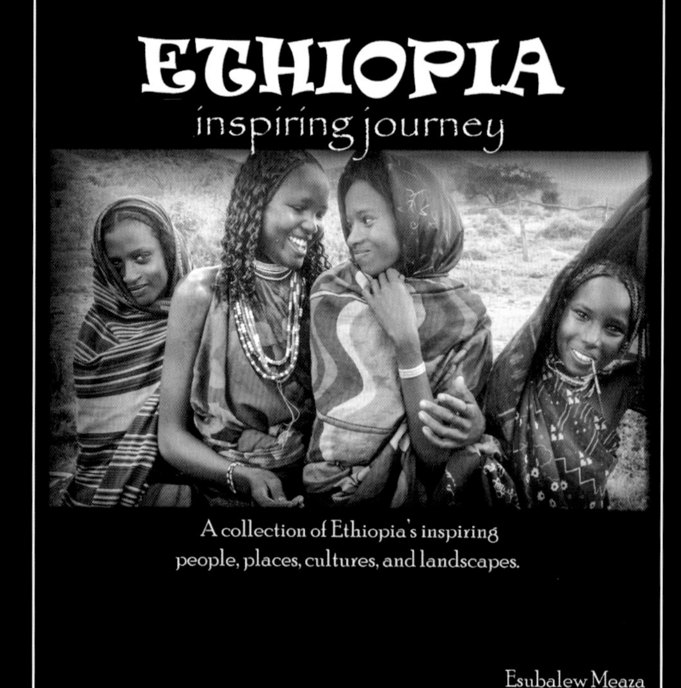

ETHIOPIA
inspiring journey
A collection of Ethiopia's inspiring
people, places, cultures, and landscapes.
Esubalew Meaza

Addis Ababa, The New Flower of Africa gives a new perspective on Ethiopia's capital city. This coffee table book highlights the positive aspects of the city and describes its history, allure, progress, and realities. It also introduces Ethiopia's many other tourist attractions, and is thus a fitting companion to the author's recently published coffee table book, *Ethiopia: Inspiring Journey.*

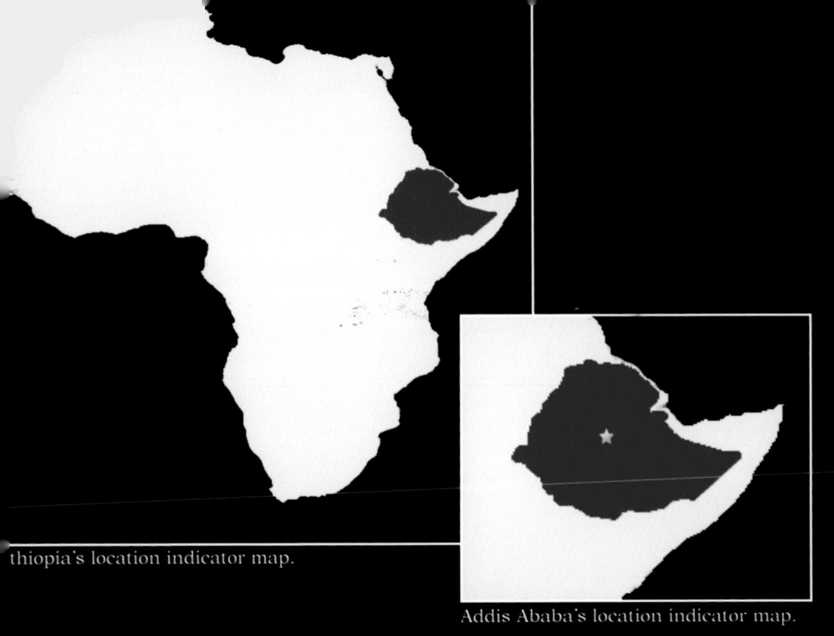

thiopia's location indicator map.

Addis Ababa's location indicator map.

Introduction

Addis Ababa is the capital city of Ethiopia. It lies close to the central highlands, at an altitude of 2,400 meters. The surrounding mountains—Mount Entoto to the north, Mount Yerer to the east, Mount Mengesha, and Mount Wechecha to the west and southwest— provide a dramatic backdrop from every angle.

Addis Ababa was founded in the late 1800s, when Emperor Menelik II, relocated his military base to the strategically advantageous peak of the Entoto Mountain. The climate there was cold and damp, therefore Empress Taitu was drawn to the Finfine plains, the land at the foothills of the mountain where the weather was mild and a nearby area called Filwoha included a hot spring. The Empress deemed the site worthy of being the new city, to be called Addis Ababa. Thus, a city was born.

Addis Ababa at its formation

The history of the city has become tied to its role as the capital city. In its more than 128 years in that role, Addis Ababa has developed into a unique federal city. Because it was created to be the seat of government, it has always been embroiled in political maneuvering and continues to serve as the default national stage for the country's social, political, and intellectual development.

The words Addis Ababa are from Ethiopia's official language, Amharic. The words translate literally to "new flower." Although the city is officially known as Addis Ababa, affectionate alternatives such as Sheger, Finfine, and Addis are commonly used.

Travelers for business or pleasure enjoy Africa's bustling and vibrant capital city. Its ethnically diverse population of more than 3.2 million is known for hospitality and a readiness to help travelers create experiences that will become long-lasting memories. Museums display Ethiopia's rich cultures, and the historic landmarks, monuments and cultural institutions bring out the city's character and charm.

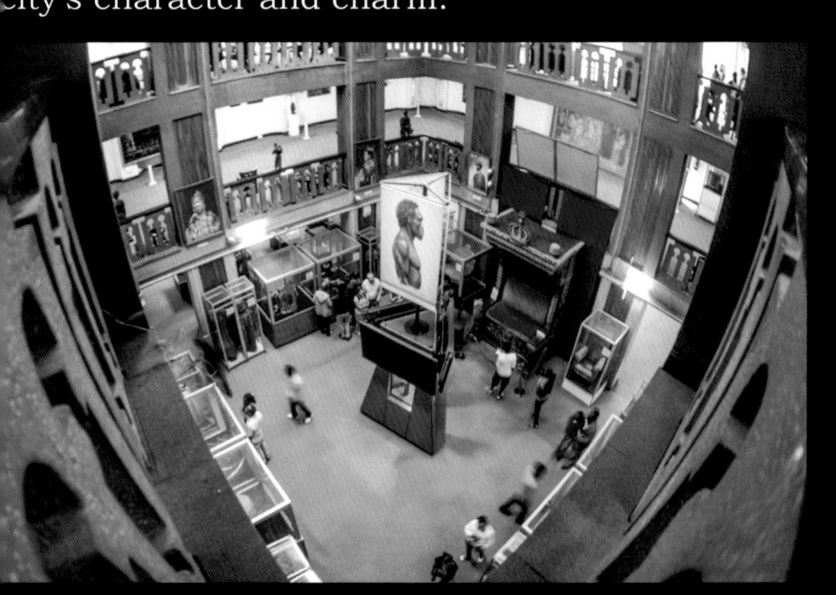

In the 1940s, the city's character expanded to include its role as a political power center of the African continent, cultivating the growing interest in cooperation among African nations.

The founders of the Organization of African Unity (OAU) envisioned Addis Ababa as a political center where African nations could discuss cooperation, sovereignty, and the promotion of solidarity among themselves. As the organization celebrates more than 50 years of existence, it continues to affirm the city as the historical and rightful place to achieve its new and refined objectives.

The African Union (AU) is a newer organization carved out of the original OAU. The new group sets missions geared toward addressing the continent's current needs. As the AU's ideological transformation is envisioned and sought, the location of its headquarters has remained. Thus, Addis Ababa's growing status as Africa's diplomatic hub has been re-asserted with a strikingly modern new building to serve as the Union's headquarters and conference center.

The city is captivating, but equally so is the wide-open countryside. A picture of serenity framed by a graceful mountain backdrop greets those who explore the natural beauty found beyond the metropolis. The towns of Akaki and Debre Zeit to the south, Sebeta and Addis Alem to the west, Debre Berhan to the northeast, and Fiche to the north await, with farms that stretch to the horizon, spectacular mountain ranges, calm rivers, and beautiful landscapes.

Addis Ababa is divided into 10 sub-cities and is home to a population of over 3.2 million inhabitants.

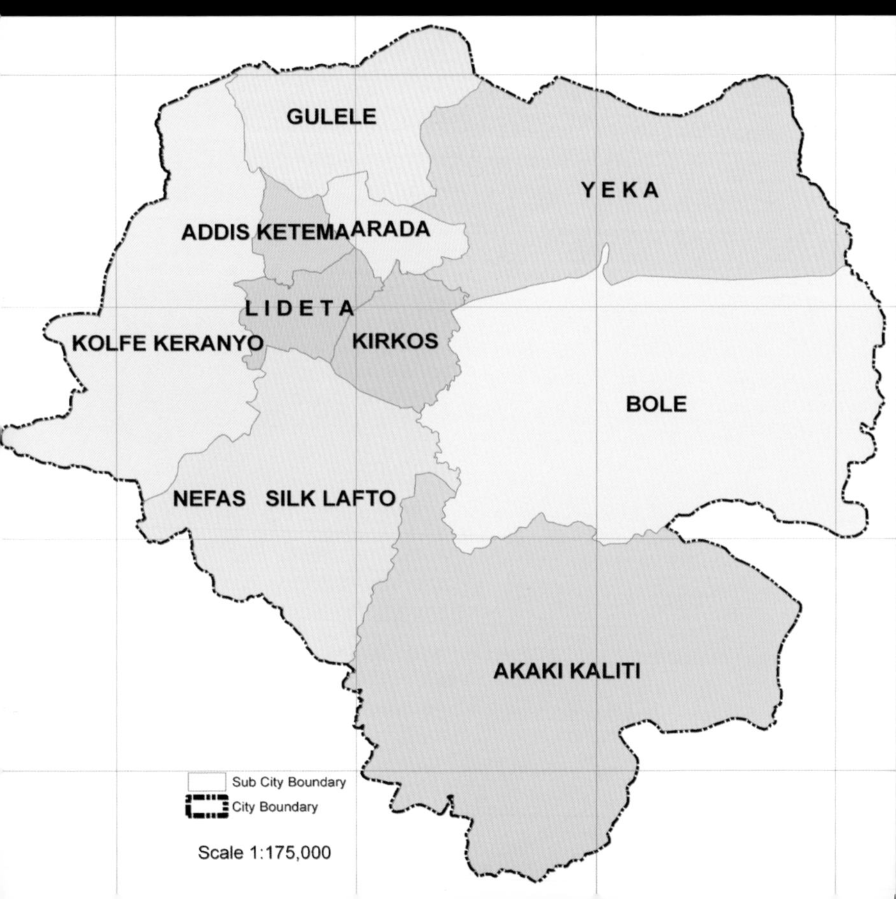

Sub cities of Addis Ababa

- **ADDIS KETEMA**
  Area : 7.41 sq.km
  Population : 271,644
- **AKAKI KALITI**
  Area: 118.08 sq.km
  Population: 195,273
- **ARADA**
  Area: 9.91 sq.km
  Population: 225,999
- **BOLE**
  Area: 122.08 sq.km
  Population: 328,900
- **GULELE**
  Area : 30.18 sq.km
  Population : 284,865
- **KIRKOS**
  Area : 14.62 sq.km
  Population : 235,441
- **KOLFE KERANYO**
  Area : 61.25 sq.km
  Population : 546,219
- **LIDETA**
  Area : 9.18 sq.km
  Population : 214,769
- **NEFAS SILK LAFTO**
  Area : 68.3 sq.km
  Population : 335,740
- **YEKA***
  Area : 81.3 sq.km
  Population : 314,000

Source of statistical data: City government of Addis Ababa

Map source: Ethiopian Mapping Agency

Addis Ababa city map with sub-city indicators

Above left: Emperor Menelik II. Above right: The palace of Emperor Menelik II and Empress Taitu, built in 1883, using traditional methods, with wooden beams, a thatched roof, and mud walls.

THE ROYAL PRESENCE

Timeless classics and witnesses to a long history, some of Africa's oldest royal residences are located in Ethiopia. From the ancient stone ruins of the Queen of Sheba's palace in Axum to the elaborate compound in Gonder and Emperor Yohannes' palace in Mekele, Ethiopia's palaces were built to affirm power, wealth, and territory. Addis Ababa is home to palaces with a comparatively short history, yet equal reverence. Although the 3,000 year old Ethiopian monarchy ended in 1974 with the downfall of Emperor Haile Selassie I, the remnants of that period are visible in and around the city. From Menelik's temporary home at the top of the Entoto Mountain to Haile Selassie's relatively young Jubilee Palace, the city is dotted with reminders of the time and people who lived during that era.

Emperor Menelik II

Empress Taitu

The Reign of Emperor Menelik II, 1889-1913

The coronation of Empress Zewditu

The Reign of Empress Zewditu, 1916-1930

Emperor Haile Selassie

Empress Menen Asfaw

The Reign of Haile Selassie I, 1930-1974

Lij Eyasu Michael

Emperor Designate: 1913-1916

Inside the Genete Leul Palace, there is a small museum containing artifacts from the reign of the late Emperor Haile Selassie I. These include his bedroom set (shown above), his imperial crown, his coronation robes, various military uniforms, and a vast number of foreign and domestic medals. Opposite page top: National Palace. Opposite page bottom: Emperor Haile Selassie I.

Imperial Palace

The Imperial is a grand compound commonly known as both the Gebbi and Menelik Palace. The palace was built by Emperor Menelik II and used as the seat of power by Ethiopia's monarchs. The compound includes Elfin, a living and guest reception area; Segannet, a balcony overlooking the city; Adarash, a hall; and other working buildings. Today it contains the offices and residence of the prime minister.

Genete Leul Palace

Emperor Haile Selassie I built the Genete Leul (Paradise of the Prince) palace in 1935. The palace was initially known as the new Gebbi, referencing the original Gebbi, the Imperial Palace, that he had occupied prior to his move.

During the brief Italian occupation of Ethiopia, the palace served as administrative headquarters for two successive Italian viceroys (*Encyclopaedia Aethiopica, D-HA, p. 691*). In 1941, the Emperor reclaimed the palace upon his return from exile. When he moved to the Jubilee Palace he donated the Genete Leul to be part of the nation's first university, known today as Addis Ababa University.

NATIONAL PALACE

Built in 1955, the Jubilee Palace was the residence of Ethiopia's last emperor, Haile Selassie I. Built to commemorate the 25th anniversary of his coronation, the palace became his primary residence from 1961 to 1974. After his dethronement in 1974, the new government renamed the palace the National Palace, and the current government continues to refer to it by this name. Today it is occupied by the current president, Dr. Mulatu Teshome, who uses it as an official and ceremonial venue to welcome state guests and foreign dignitaries.

There are two unique and historical churches on Entoto, the towering mountain situated to the north of Addis Ababa: Entoto Maryam
St. Mary of Entoto, shown above) and St. Raguel-Elias (shown on opposite page). Visiting them and the museums within thei

Saint Mary of Entoto

If a city had parents, Addis Ababa would undoubtedly belong to Emperor Menelik II and Empress Taitu, and the Entoto Mountain would be its birthplace. Today, a short drive from the city center leads to the highest mountain in Addis Ababa and the site of Emperor Menelik's former capital. Crowning the top of the mountain is the first church of Addis Ababa, Entoto Maryam, which also hosted the coronation of Emperor Menelik as King of Kings. The Entoto Museum located within the gates of the church further provides an enriching experience with timeless photographs, the couple's household effects, and artifacts used in the Battle of Adwa. Behind the church is a private compound with the Emperor's palace and living quarters.

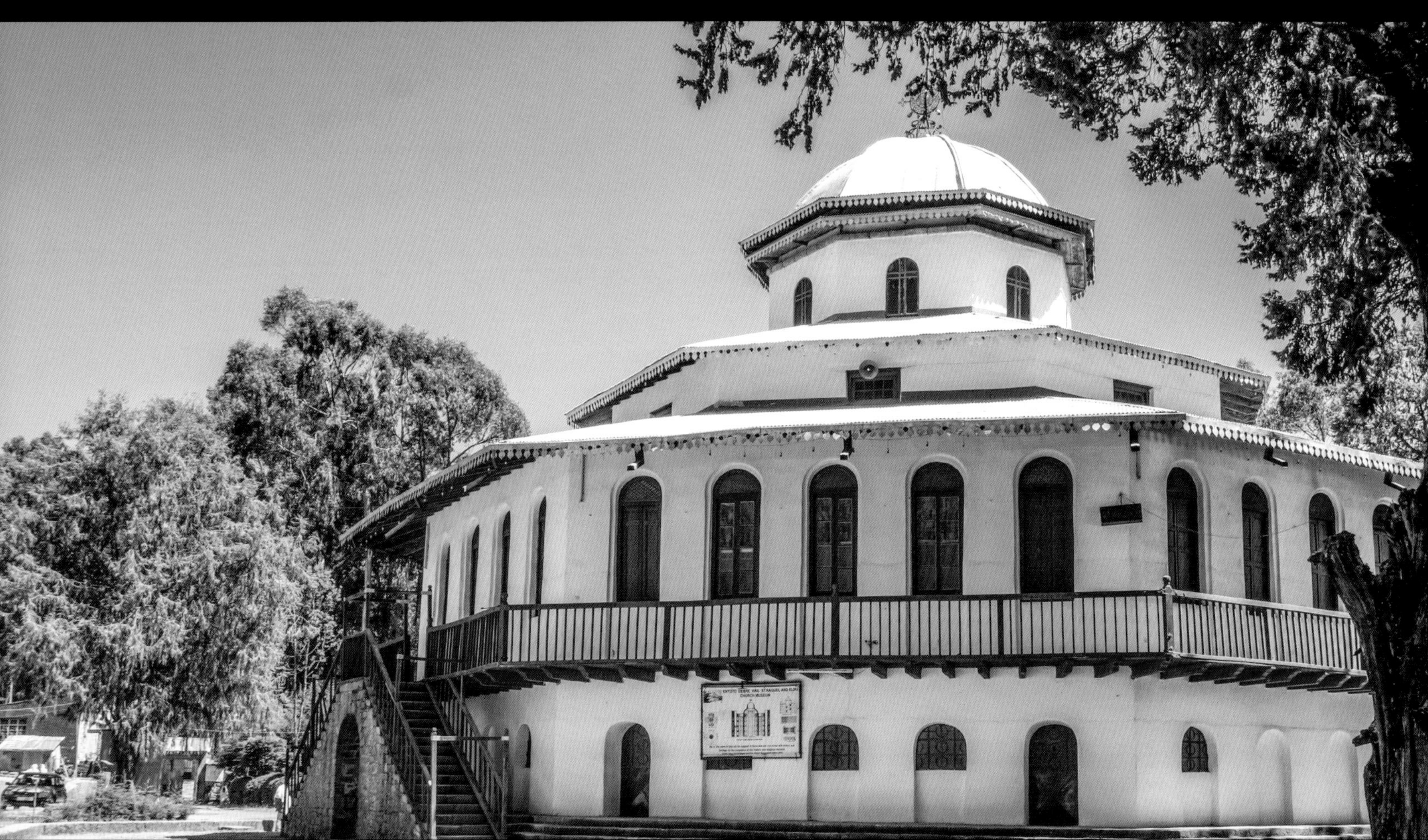

Saint Raguel Church

Saint Raguel is the second church built near the top of the Entoto Mountain within the compound of Emperor Menelik II. Its construction began in 1885, and the church was inaugurated November 5, 1889 (*Encyclopaedia Aethiopica, D-HA, p.322*). One of two churches dominating the ridge with its white arched architecture, Saint Raguel's imposing presence is a treat from the old times. The inside of the church is filled with a multitude of Ethiopian-style religious paintings telling various stories of the Bible.

SHEIKH OJALE'S PALACE

Born in 1817 in the city of Komosha, Sheikh Ojale Al-Hasan is known to have been an Ethiopian warrior and a champion of unity. His palace dates back to the beginning of the 20th-century, after Ojale had become ruler of the town of Assosa and had helped the military expedition led by the central government to conquer Benishangul region, in 1897-1898 (*Old Tracks in the New Flower*, p.99).

FRANCO-ETHIOPIAN RAILWAY

In the late 1800s and early 1900s, Addis Ababa was the site of many modern structures. Among them were the Bank of Abyssinia, the Taitu Hotel, the first hospital, and the Franco-Ethiopian railway, connecting the port country of Djibouti to Addis Ababa. The construction of the 784 kilometers of the Franco-Ethiopian Railway line started in Djibouti in 1897 and was completed twenty years later, when the rail tracks reached Addis Ababa in 1917.

The resting terminal/house for travelers was named after the governor of French Somaliland, Leonce Lagarde, who signed a treaty with Emperor Menelik II to make Djibouti City the designated port for Ethiopia's growing foreign commerce and communications (*Encyclopaedia Aethiopica, O-X, p.324*). Today the terminal and area at one end of Churchill Road is named after Governor Lagarde.

Top: Legehar terminal. Above: Legehar terminal at its formation.

TAITU HOTEL

Taitu Hotel was established in 1889. As the first hotel in the country, it introduced a new culture of guest services and accommodation. Located in the heart of the city in an area called Piassa, the Taitu Hotel continued to offer travelers accommodations until January 2015, when the hotel's upper level was destroyed by a fire. Although the lower level café has resumed service, a complete restoration is expected.

Top: Off the wide and open main lobby, a grand wooden staircase leads to rooms on the upper level. Left: The gracefully decorated main dining area is home to the famous daily lunch buffet.

FINFINE ADARASH

Located just beyond the National Palace, the Finfine Adarash is a historic site with direct access to the Filwoha, a boiling hot mineral water recognized for its ability to help one recover, relax, and rejuvenate. The mineral water is also said to have inspired Empress Taitu and Emperor Menelik II to relocate the capital from the Entoto Mountain to the lush valley below.

In the early 1930s during Haile Selassie's reign, the spa facilities were further improved, and a new hotel initially named Hotel d'Europe was opened. Today the hotel is known by one of the city's affectionate names, Finfine. The warm and inviting garden, the deep-healing hot mineral spring water bath and the elegant historic restaurant, are just a few reasons to visit the Finfine Adarash.

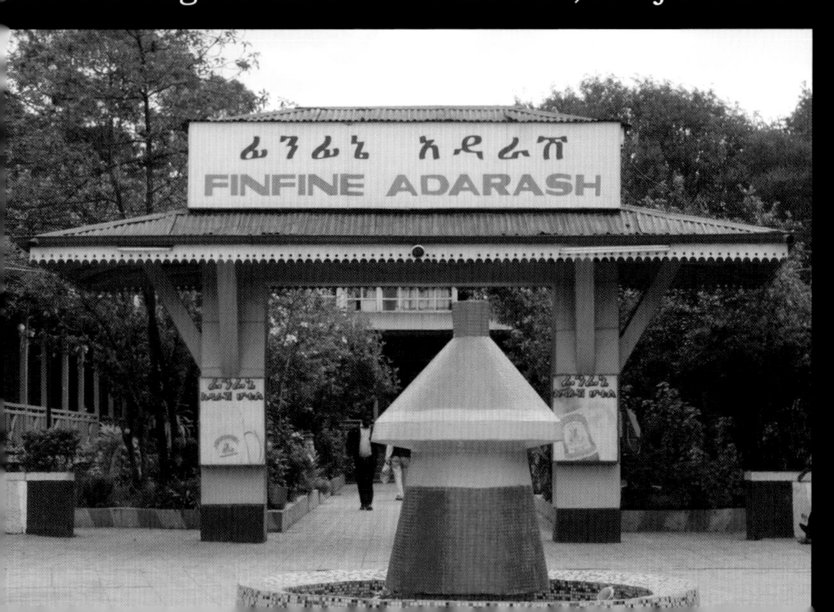

Above: The exterior front view of the Holy Trinity Cathedral. Below: The dome paintings inside the Holy Trinity Cathedral graced by voluminous crystal chandelier. Opposite page: Inside the Holy Trinity Cathedra

HOLY TRINITY CATHEDRAL

Holy Trinity Cathedral, known in Amharic as Kidist Selassie, is a cathedral located in an area called Arat Kilo. The cathedral was dedicated to the British officers and other ranks who, together with Ethiopian patriots sacrificed their lives for the liberation of Ethiopia. Emperor Haile Selassie I laid the cathedral's cornerstone in 1930, but construction work was suspended during the Italian occupation and resumed in 1941. The eclectic European-style cathedral was inaugurated on the 16th of January 1944.

The inside of the building is as intriguing as its unique exterior design. The elaborate chandelier descending from the ceiling near the Mekdes (the most inner sanctuary of the church) brings attention to the murals around it. When turned on, the lights illuminate the murals, which depict Christ ascending to heaven free from the cross and presiding over the final Day of Judgment. The stunning architecture, combined with the carvings, mosaics, and meaningfully decorative stained glass windows evoke emotions of admiration for the details and beauty. Among the artwork displayed are the depiction of Ethiopia's own Saint Abuna Tekle Haymanot, Saint George, and other saints.

Inside the Holy Trinity Cathedral

Above: The royal thrones inside the Holy Trinity Cathedral. Below: Stained glass windows bringing inspiration and joy from Ethiopia's Saint Abune Takla-Haymanot, Saint George, the depiction of Jesus' crucifixion, and other Biblical scenes. Opposite page top The crypts of Emperor Haile Selassie and Empress Menen Asfaw located inside the Holy Trinity Cathedral. Opposite page bottom Memorial grave statue of the legendary Ethiopian singer, Tilahun Gessesse.

The Holy Trinity Cathedral is not only one of the holiest places to visit when in Addis Ababa, but it is also a keeper of some of the nation's extraordinary historical artifacts. Throne chairs used by the emperor and his wife, Empress Menen Asfaw, are permanently positioned directly in front of the Mekdes, the holiest of the holy parts of the church.

The Holy Trinity Cathedral is also the final resting place of emperors, military heroes, religious leaders, famous entertainers, and many historical figures. Among those whose burial place is here: Emperor Haile Selassie I and his wife, Empress Menen Asfaw, the late Prime Minister Meles Zenawi, and the king of Ethiopian music, Tilahun Gessesse.

Monuments

Addis Ababa has many monuments that serve as memorials for its history. Each offers an interesting and enriching experience to visitors. In addition to being standing witnesses, the monuments tell the story of Ethiopia from the perspective of the Ethiopian people.

The monuments of Addis Ababa are also teaching objects used to invoke thoughts and start discussions. They challenge new generations to look back at the achievements and trials of their ancestors.

Letters on the city's map are used to identify the locations of the monuments.

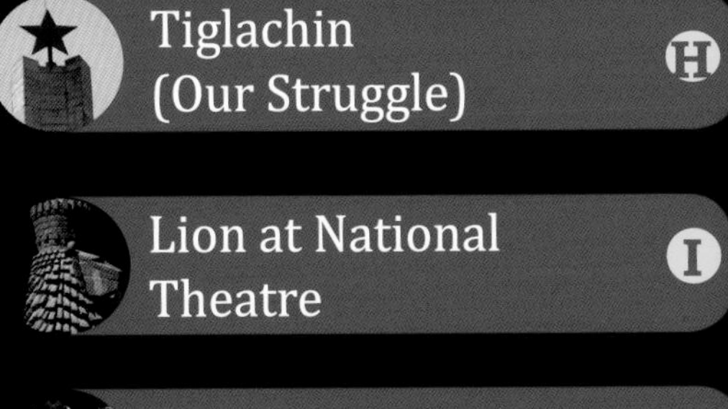

Due to light rail construction, some monuments may have been temporarily moved.

Emperor Tewodros Circle

A circle is dedicated to Emperor Tewodros, who ruled Ethiopia from 1855-1868. Born Kassa Hailu, the emperor is widely credited for his attempt to unify the country and introduce Ethiopia to the modern world. At the center of the circle is a replica of a cannon, a prime example of Tewodros's early understanding of modernization. The cannon, named Sebastopol, was the flagship of the cannons the emperor ordered a group of visiting European missionary crafts-men to construct. Although perplexed by his order at first, the craftsmen were able to rise to the challenge, eventually making his vision a reality.

Korea War Veterans Memorial

Ethiopian Korean War Veterans Memorial is dedicated to the Ethiopian fighters who fought gallantly in the Chuncheon region for the cause of world peace and freedom during the Korean War (1951-1953). In the war, 122 Ethiopians lost their lives, and 536 were wounded.

ABUNE PETROS

Abune Petros paid the ultimate pric
for refusing to accept the Fascis
Italian leadership during its five-yea
occupation of Ethiopia. The monu
ment, built a few steps from the sit
of his brutal execution, was erected ir
1941 to commemorate him and others
who became martyrs of the resistance
against the Italian occupation. The
original statue, with full bishopric
robe and a Bible was replaced by one
with a chain and gun, highlighting the
Italians' vicious treatment and Abune
Petros's deep convictions.

Abune Petros was born in 1882 in Fiche, a towr
120 kilometers from Addis Ababa. Ordained as
a bishop in 1928 at Saint Mark Monastery ir
Alexandria, Egypt, he died on July 30, 1936, ir
AA. The above photo shows the headstone marking the location of his brutal execution.

THE MONUMENT OF MARTYRS

February 19, Yekatit 12 on the Ethiopian calendar, was a Friday. Notables and ordinary people rose early to flock to the ceremony at the Little Gebbi (*Anthony Mockler, Haile Selassie's War*). Among the people who attended were two young Ethiopians, Abraha Deboch and Mogus Asgedom. As the ceremony commenced, the order to salute the Duce of Fascimo, Benito Mussolini, was returned with a surprising rain of grenades. The three-day retaliation to this attempt to assassinate Mussolini's military commander, Viceroy Rodolfo Graziani, makes Yekatit 12 (February 19, 1937) a dark day in Addis Ababa's history. The city was set aflame and many of its residents were killed.

> The federal secretary, Guido Cortese gave this order: "Today is the day when we should show our devotion to our Victory by reacting and destroying the Ethiopians for three days. For three days I gave you the carte Blanche to destroy and kill and do what you want to the Ethiopians."

The indiscriminate massacre, and imprisonment of Ethiopians by the Italian forces made Yekatit 12 both a day of terror and the turning point for Ethiopians' determination, delivering new strength to the resistance movement. The monument of the martyrs was erected in 1942 as a reminder to citizens

Star of Victory

This medal commemorates the Ethiopian 1941 victory over Italian forces. The obverse is in Amharic with the same message on the reverse in English, recognizing the role of Britain in helping to oust the invading forces.

The Freedom Monument

The Freedom Monument is a memorial located at the intersection of Adwa, Queen Elizabeth, and Development Through Cooperation Avenues in Arat Kilo. It is considered an important symbol of freedom and commemorates the 1941 victory of the Ethiopians over the Italians. The memorial also honors the Ethiopians who perished resisting the invading Fascist forces between 1936 and 1941. As a permanent reminder of the five-year struggle, the history is carved on stone tablets around the monument so that generations can meet and take in firsthand accounts of the events.

Opposite page: Miazia 27 is the official name of the square where the Freedom Monument is located in. The monument commemorates that date in 1933 in the Ethiopian calendar when the country was liberated from the invading Fascist forces.

Tiglachin Monument

Tiglachin is a multipart monument inaugurated in 1984 and dedicated to the men and women who gave their lives in the cross-border war with Somalia. The monument is a fifty-meter-tall triangular column located in a 30,000-square-meter park in front of the Black Lion Hospital on Churchill Road.

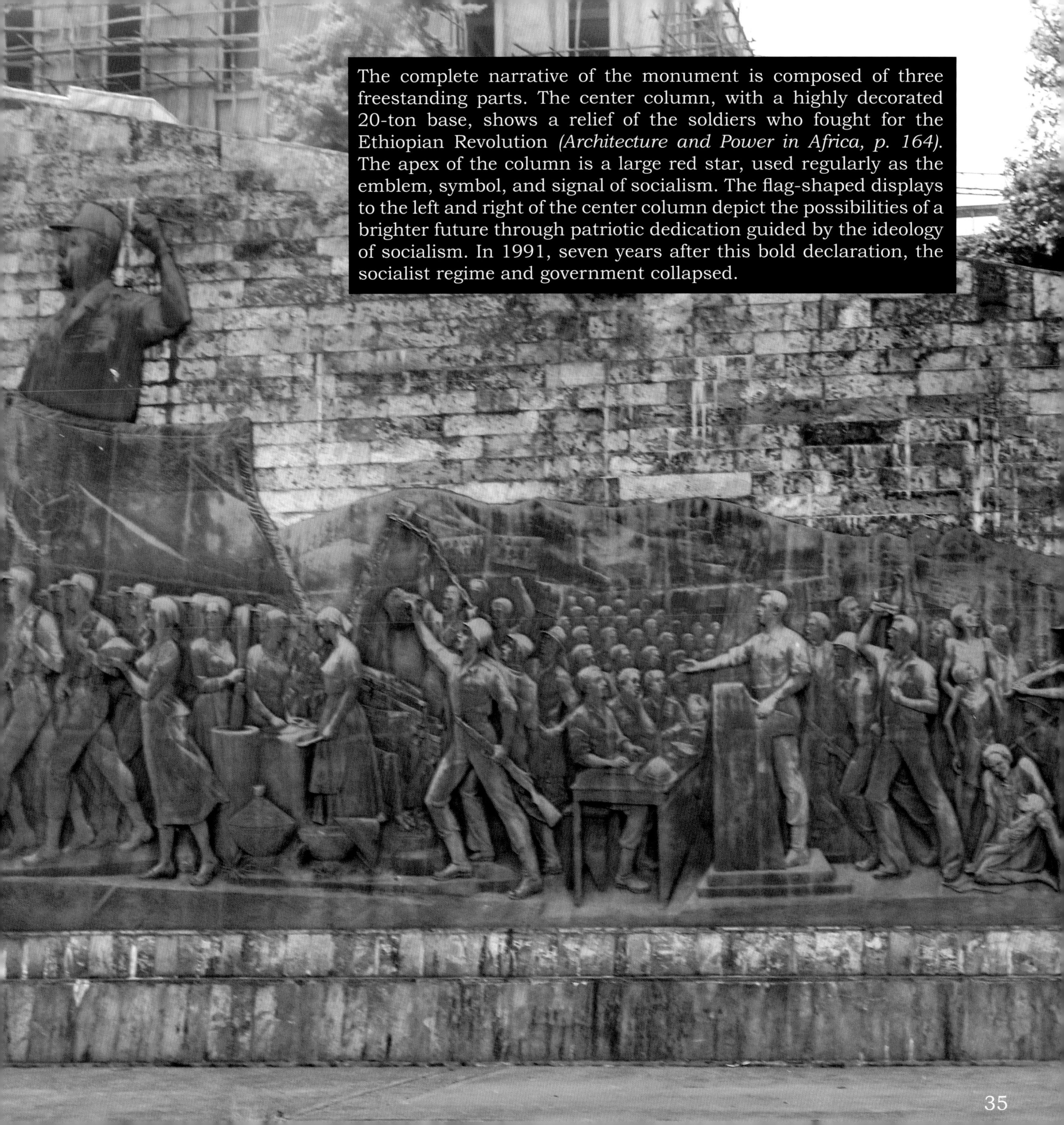

The complete narrative of the monument is composed of three freestanding parts. The center column, with a highly decorated 20-ton base, shows a relief of the soldiers who fought for the Ethiopian Revolution *(Architecture and Power in Africa, p. 164).* The apex of the column is a large red star, used regularly as the emblem, symbol, and signal of socialism. The flag-shaped displays to the left and right of the center column depict the possibilities of a brighter future through patriotic dedication guided by the ideology of socialism. In 1991, seven years after this bold declaration, the socialist regime and government collapsed.

Lion of Judah

The Lion of Judah is a symbol of the Israelite tribe of Judah. The symbol has been adopted to represent the Ethiopian state and monarchy. It has its basis in the Book of Revelation (5:5), representing Jesus. The Lion of Judah statue on the left is located in front of the Ethiopian National Theater and the one shown above is located in front of Ethio-Djibouti Railway Legehar terminal.

Emperor Menelik II

In Menelik II Square stands the imposing equestrian statue (shown on opposite page) of the emperor that affirms the victory of his people during the Battle of Adwa in 1896. The statue is a reminder of the Ethiopians' determination and their defiance at submitting to a foreign power. Located near Saint George's church, the statue of Menelik II riding his horse, Abba Dagnew, is gazing north in the direction of the mountains of Adwa.

The statue was built by the order of Empress Zewditu, the daughter of Emperor Menelik II, in memory of her father, and was inaugurated by Emperor Haile Selassie I.

MUSEUMS

he Addis Ababa Museum is known not only for its collection of rt and artifacts depicting the evolution of the city, but also for the uilding's magnificent structure and historical importance. It was once he home of the Honorable Ras (Duke) Birru Wolde-Gabriel, who was war minster during Emperor Menelik's administration. The house vas turned into a museum in 1986 to commemorate Addis Ababa's 00th birthday. The Museum's timeless elegance is a reflection of its ntrinsic, historical, and artistic value stored in it.

he architectural detail and decorative elements of the building make a perfect entryway to the Museum's large collection of objects. The listressed facade and peeling yellow exterior paint assimilate the nuseum into the surrounding trees and manicured garden. The charm f the multi-paneled windows further enhances the look while under-mphasizing sporadically missing pieces. Visitors can take advantage f these missing panels to snap a close-up picture of the exterior's rtistic beauty.

he Museum, located near Meskel Square, has seven methodically ivided sections, each possessing materials of significance from the ity's long history. The display walks through the city's early develop-nental period and shows its gradual transformation over 100 years to s present-day metropolis status.

he first section of the museum, Finfine Hall, captures the beginning f the city through photographs, paintings, and other materials. mong the many reminders of the city's early times are the portraits f Emperor Menelik II and Empress Taitu in their coronation robes.

he second section, Edget Hall, builds upon the knowledge from infine Hall by introducing the developmental era of the city. Photos of ioneer music bands, the first hotel, and the first telephone apparatus re a few of the things one encounters in Edget Hall.

he Swiss engineer Alfred Ilg was a close confidant to Emperor Menelik . His position gave him exposure to take memorable photographs of ddis Ababa. Alfred Ilg Hall is the next section in the museum and ncludes pictures of the city and Ilg's residence.

he fourth hall in the museum is Adwa Hall. Adwa is a city located in ne northern part of Ethiopia. Artifacts of various levels of importance, ncluding weapons used in the Adwa war, are displayed in this hall

Above: Large-sized paintings of the founders of Addis Ababa, Emperor Menelik II and Empress Taitu, welcoming visitors as they enter the Finfine Hall of the Addis Ababa Museum. Below: A painting depicting the Adwa war

The collection of handcrafts and contemporary arts located in the next two halls are frozen-in-time representations of the intellectual and physical capabilities of Addis Ababa residents. In addition to tangible examples of handcrafts, pictures of individuals crafting augment one's understanding of the depicted time's reality. The museum concludes by presenting modern times through the Centenary Hall.

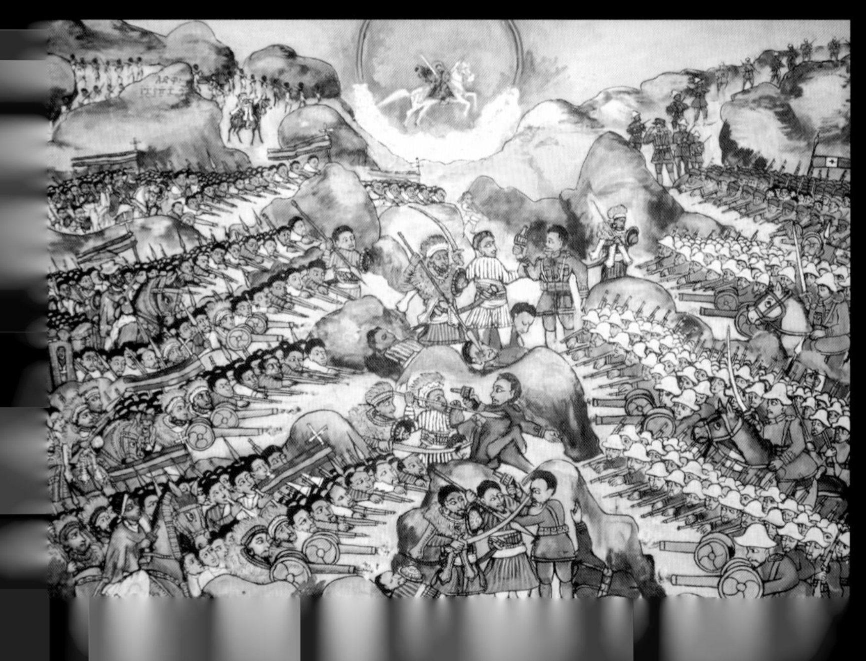

Affection of Music

The Affection of Music sculpture, located in the Modern Art Hall in the Addis Ababa Museum, depicts a person's love of music through his attachment to his single-stringed bowed lute, a musical instrument known as a *masinko*.

RED TERROR
Martyrs Memorial Museum

The Red Terror Martyrs Memorial Museum is located few steps from Meskel square, Addis Ababa's main public square. The museum commemorates the victims of a dark period in Ethiopia's recent history. Red Terror refers to a campaign of torture and mass killings between 1977 and 1978, during the Derg regime.

The museum was unveiled on March 7, 2010 by Kebebushe Admasu, a mother who lost four of her teenage children on the same day during the Red Terror. As you enter the front door, an inscription with a quotation that summarizes her pain and agony awaits: "As if I bore them all in one night, they slew them in a single night."

Displays at the Red Terror Museum include: Photos and names of victims, personal artifacts of the victims and cabinets filled with human skeletons.

At the entrance plaza of the museum stands a status of three women consumed with intolerable melancholy. The plaque on the base of the statue reads: Never, Ever Again.

NATIONAL MUSEUM OF ETHIOPIA

Addis Ababa is home to some of Ethiopia's best museums, where one can discover a wealth of artifacts and exhibitions. The National Museum of Ethiopia, located in Amist Kilo, is known for its thought-provoking presentations of Ethiopia's treasures. It is also a place where visitors learn about the richness and diversity of Ethiopian culture. However, it would hardly be an exaggeration to say that the visiting public associates this museum first and foremost with its famous resident, *Lucy*.

The National Museum was established in 1944 with a few archeological collections, ethnographic objects, and artifacts donated by Emperor Haile Selassie I. The museum exhibits are arranged in four sections: Prehistory, Historical and Archaeological Findings, Ethnography, and Modern Art. The archaeological and prehistory sections, located on the lower level of the museum, connect visitors to the very beginning of humanity. *Ardi*, *Selam*, and *Lucy* are human fossils dating back over three million years. As the home of these fossils and the oldest stone tools, Ethiopia earns the title of Cradle of Humankind, and the National Museum is the proud home of these and other ancient artifacts.

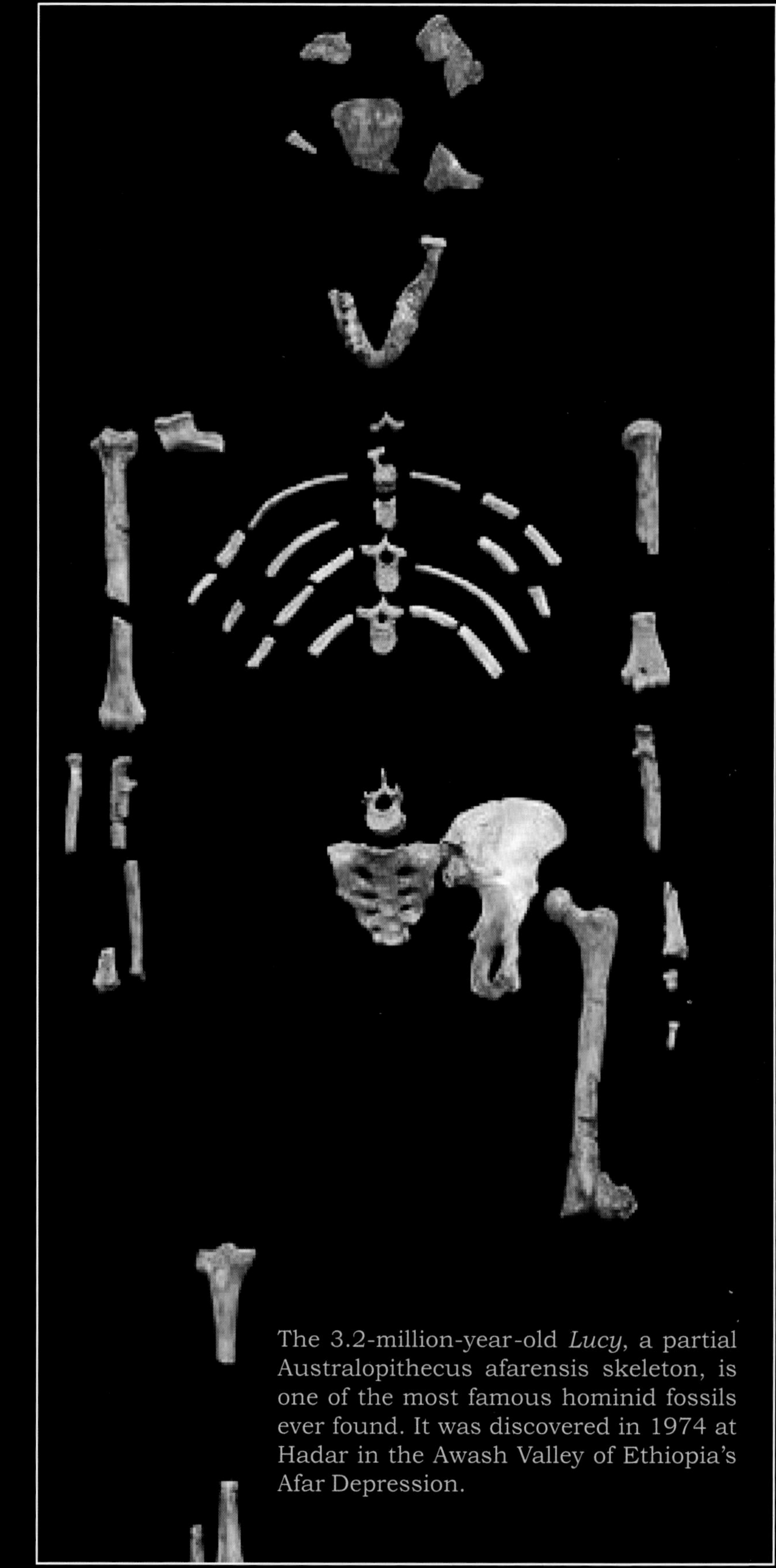

The 3.2-million-year-old *Lucy*, a partial Australopithecus afarensis skeleton, is one of the most famous hominid fossils ever found. It was discovered in 1974 at Hadar in the Awash Valley of Ethiopia's Afar Depression.

The first floor of the Museum contains objects from ancient and medieval periods, as well as ceremonial dresses and memorabilia from former rulers. Imperial crowns of Yohannes IV, Menelik II, Taitu, and Haile Selassie I are among the many objects displayed on the first floor.

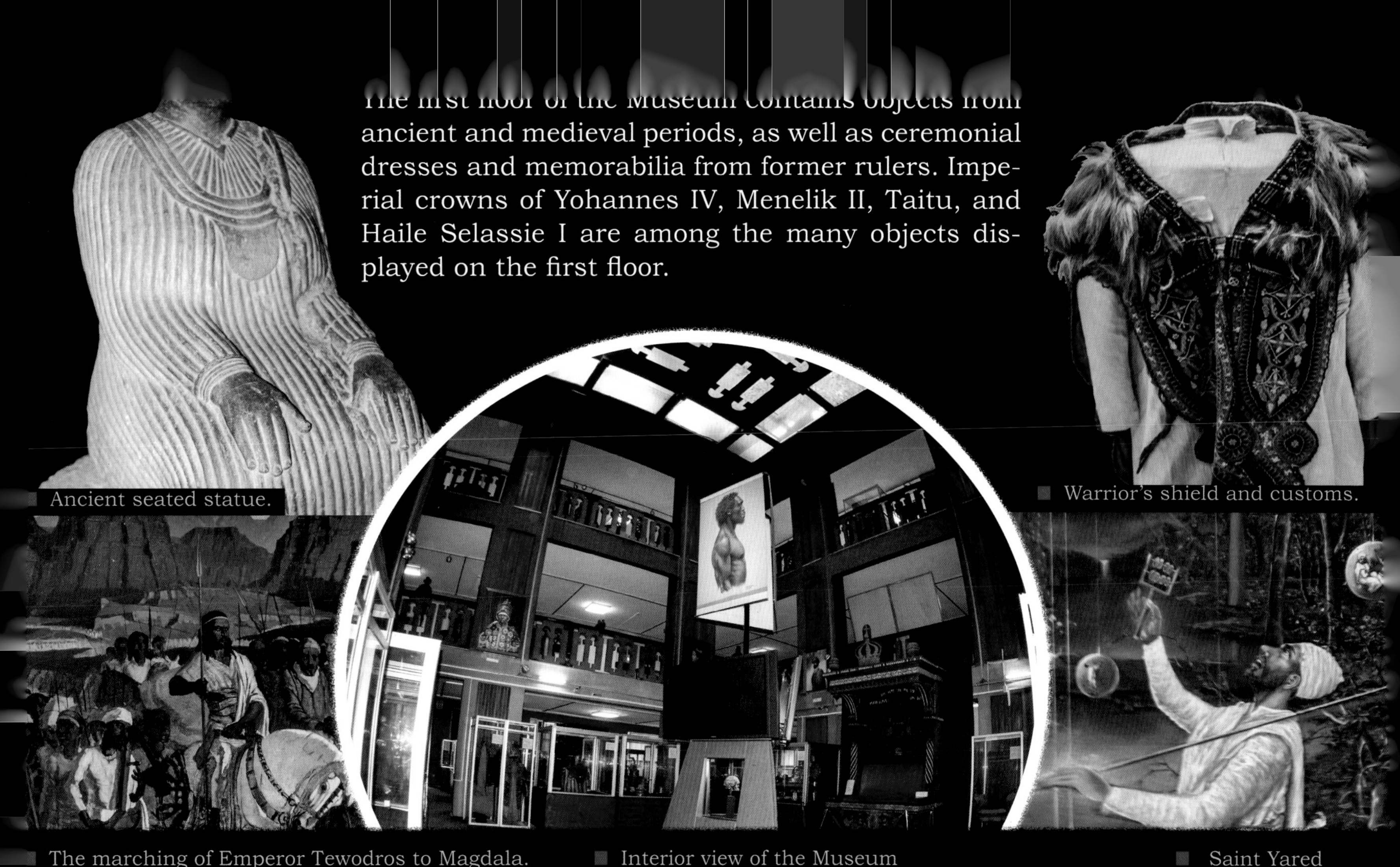

Ancient seated statue.

Warrior's shield and customs.

The marching of Emperor Tewodros to Magdala.

Interior view of the Museum

Saint Yared

The second floor displays artwork in chronological order, from traditional to contemporary works. Paintings depicting many Ethiopian legendary and popular stories are among the displays on this floor. The journey of the Queen of Sheba, the marching of Emperor Tewodros, the stories of the Bible, Demera, and the celebration of the finding of the cross are among the stories expressed through the arts exhibited on this floor.

Finally, the third floor has a comprehensive ethnographic collection. A visit to this floor is simply a journey around Ethiopia. Here, the Museum underscores Ethiopia's diverse and rich culture.

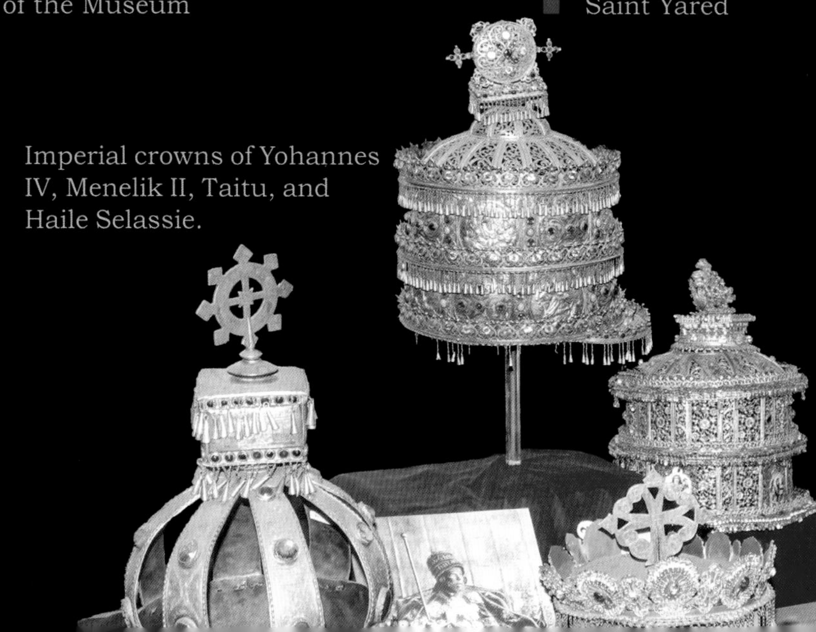

Imperial crowns of Yohannes IV, Menelik II, Taitu, and Haile Selassie.

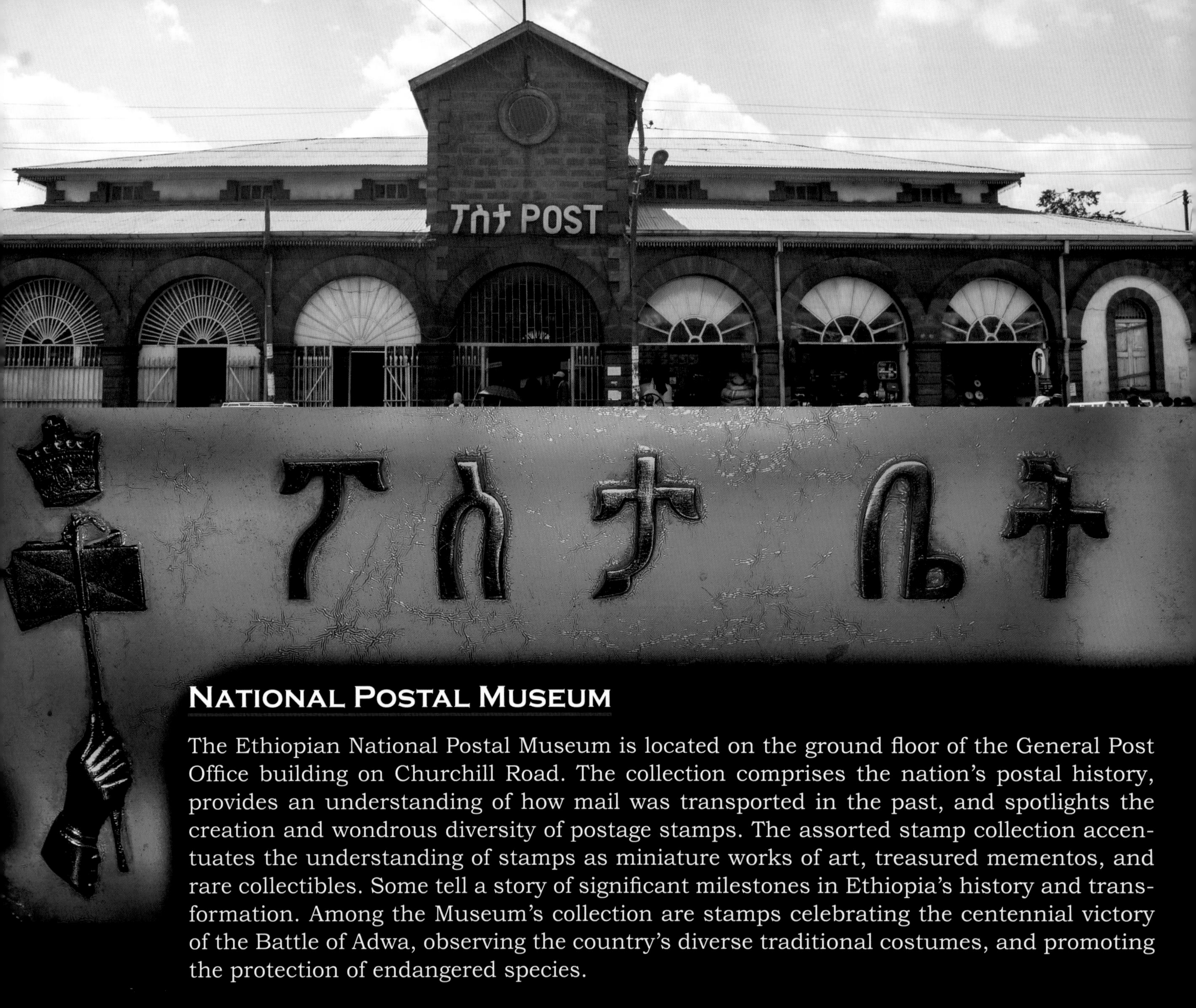

National Postal Museum

The Ethiopian National Postal Museum is located on the ground floor of the General Post Office building on Churchill Road. The collection comprises the nation's postal history, provides an understanding of how mail was transported in the past, and spotlights the creation and wondrous diversity of postage stamps. The assorted stamp collection accentuates the understanding of stamps as miniature works of art, treasured mementos, and rare collectibles. Some tell a story of significant milestones in Ethiopia's history and transformation. Among the Museum's collection are stamps celebrating the centennial victory of the Battle of Adwa, observing the country's diverse traditional costumes, and promoting the protection of endangered species.

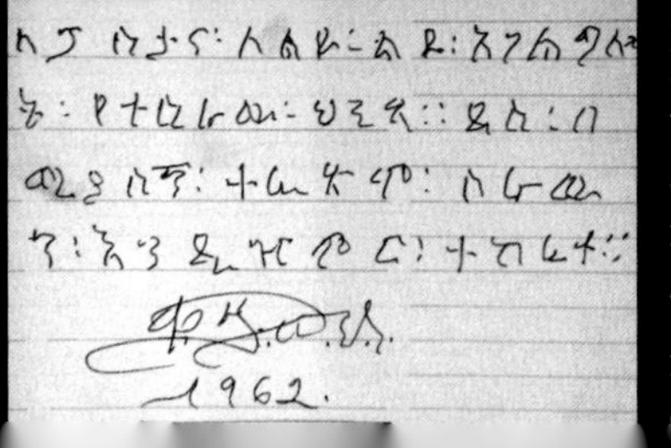

In 1970, five years before the establishment of the National Postal Museum, Emperor Haile Selassie inaugurated the new building of the Ministry of Post. His opening message (loosely translated below) and the pair of scissors used to cut the ribbons are displayed in the museum.

"The building constructed to serve as the postal office and also render other services has been successfully completed and is now open for service."

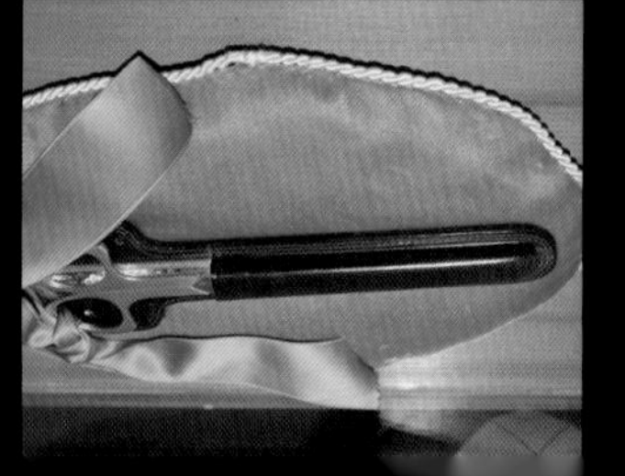

The Ethiopian National Postal Museum was opened to the public on August 19, 1975. It contains tools and equipment used by traditional postal carriers, original stamp proof drawings, catalogue-related materials, and stamps from various points of its existence.

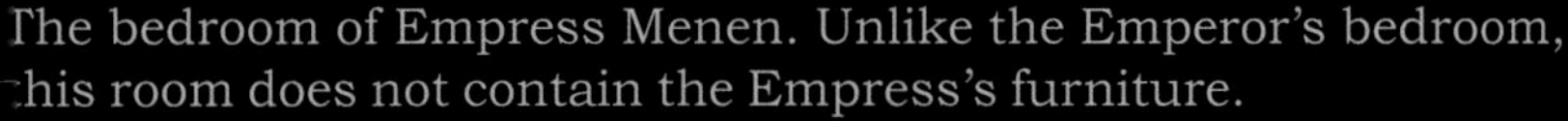

The bedroom of Empress Menen. Unlike the Emperor's bedroom, this room does not contain the Empress's furniture.

The entrance hallway to the Institute of Ethiopian Studies.

Institution of Ethiopian Studies

The Institute of Ethiopian Studies (IES) was established in 1963 at Addis Ababa University with the objective of documenting, analyzing, and disseminating knowledge about the languages, cultures, and history of Ethiopia. The museum contains more than 10,000 artifacts of historical significance.

The IES reflects Ethiopia's ethnic diversity by highlighting each group's unique identity and celebrating its way of life. Located in Leul Genet, Emperor Haile Selassie's palace, the layout of the Museum follows the story of life from birth to death and beyond, and how the different stages of life are viewed and expe-

Vivid photographs of the old Addis Ababa take visitors back in time to experience life in the city more than 100 years ago. Photographs showing the coronations of the Emperor Haile Selassie I and the unveiling of the statue of Emperor Menelik II, both of which were celebrated over several days, are among the images displayed.

The Anthropological section of the museum provides a quick visit through Ethiopia. Here, a theme of birth to death transports visitors through Ethiopia's various cultures. Such cultural marks as rites of passage, marriage, national food, household goods, death, and beliefs in the afterlife are highlighted through photos, narratives, and households.

Top right: A replica of the types of huts found in Ethiopia's Afar region is on display. Below: Waka is the Konso tribe's unique wooden burial grave marker, often telling stories about the life and status of the deceased. The Wakas shown below are located in the Death and Beyond section of the Museum.

Zoological Natural History Museum

The Zoological Natural History Museum, located in the compound of Addis Ababa University's Arat Kilo campus, was founded in 1955. Its mission is to provide knowledge and understanding, and through research programs, to study and preserve Ethiopia's natural heritage. The Museum is focused principally on exhibiting representatives of the rich variety of animal species found in Ethiopia. Currently the Museum's collection includes over 12,000 species of animals.

The Museum's permanent display of specimen collections includes about 34 of red sea corals, more than 1,100 of mammals, more than 330 of marine and freshwater mollusks, more than 800 of birds, 36 of echinoderms, more than 6,000 of insects, more than 420 of reptiles, more than 320 of fish, more than 520 of amphibians, and hundreds of species of butterflies.

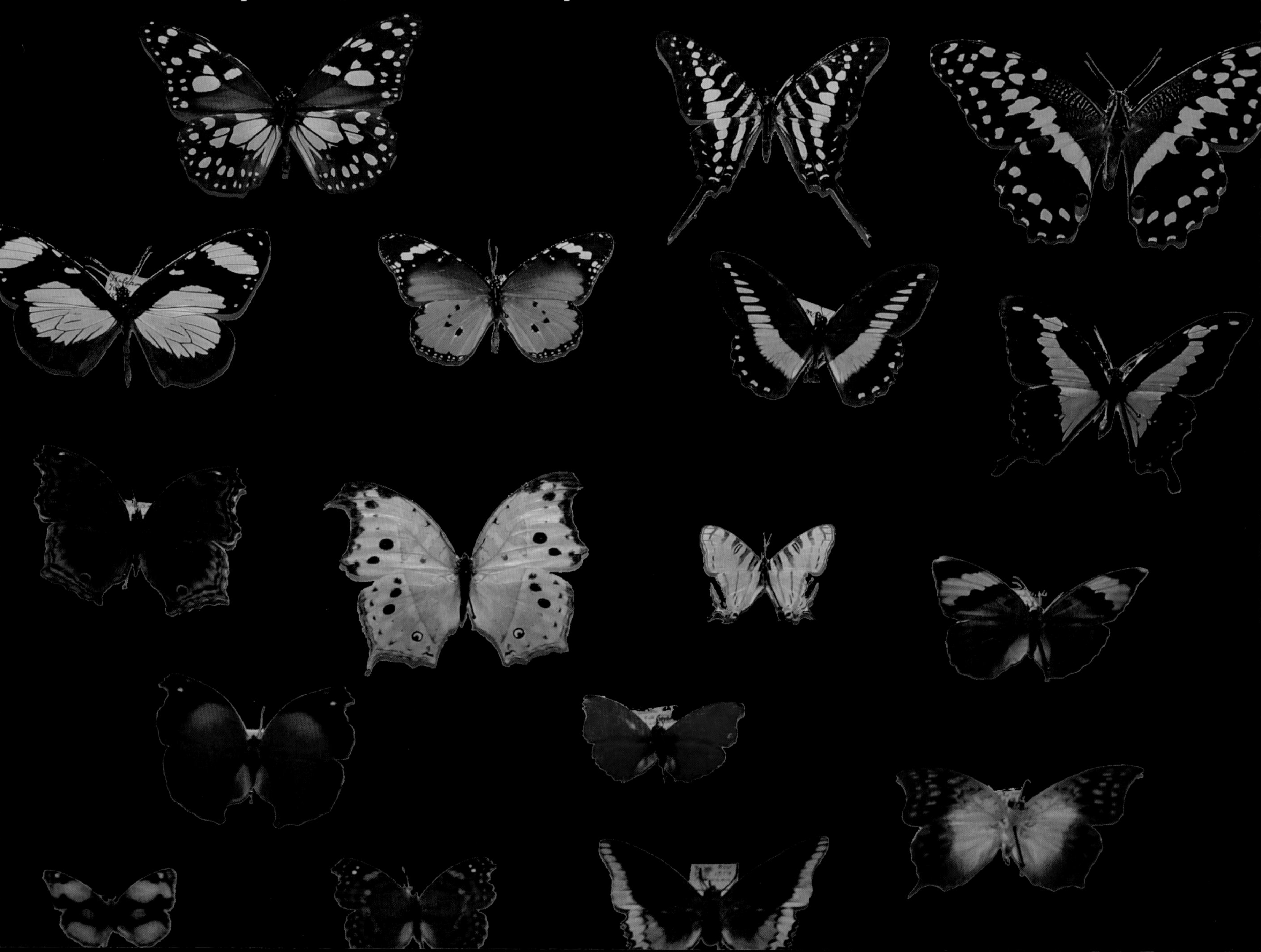

THE MINI ETHIOPIA EXHIBITS

Mini Ethiopia—The Journey Through Ethiopia permanent exhibit is a place designed to accommodate visitors with limited time. Built in the early 1970s, the museum attracts diplomats, world leaders, and business travelers by introducing them to Ethiopia's historic artifacts and locations through six thoughtfully designed and efficiently organized rooms.

Below: Partial replicas of cave carving found near Dilla (Sidamo Region), approximately 2000 BC.

Axum Room

The first room emphasizes Ethiopia as the cradle of humankind through prehistoric tools, remains and informative documents. The exit to the first room leads to the second room, the Axum section where visitors are immersed in relics, photos descriptions, and paintings depicting the Axumite Kingdom's era. The third room is about the holy city of Lalibela, known for its 11 rock-hewn churches. This section of the museum contains a bird's-eye-view model of the location of the churches.

Lalibela Room

Harar Room

The castle city of Gonder is represented in the fourth room with diagrams, descriptions, and paintings portraying the various castles and churches found in it. The fifth room highlights the Sof Omar Caves located about 120 kilometers from the city of Goba. The river of Weyeb passes through the 15-kilometer-long cave. The room is designed to mimic the feel of the cave and breathtaking natural phenomena through embedded lights, painting of the winding Weyeb river, and walls comparable to those found in an actual cave. The exhibition concludes by taking the visitor to Jegol in Harar, a walled city in eastern Ethiopia. Photographs illustrating the colorful market of Harar and replicas of interior home decorations unique to the city are displayed in this room.

Gonder Room

Sof Omar Room

Sympathy palm branches, made from an iron sheet, sent by the French president in condolences for Emperor Menelik's

The Menelik Mausoleum

The Be'ata Maryam Church, located on the compound of the Grand Palace of Menelik II, was built by order of Empress Zewditu in commemoration of her father, Emperor Menelik II. Attractively concealed under the shade of various eucalyptus, palm, and acacia trees, the church covers about 2,400 square meters of land. The exterior of the church exhibits various signs and symbols of the emperor's reign. The symbol of his crown with the initial of his first name in the Amharic language is one unequivocal hallmark of the Menelik era. The unassertive yet beautiful square stone exterior is topped with a large dome with a smaller dome of its own.

Sculptures of lions, unmistakable reminders of the imperial time, guard the entrances of the church. The paintings decorating the Qene Mahelet (the outermost section of the three concentric sections of the church) depict various achievements and events in Ethiopian history. Among them are paintings illustrating the story of the Queen of Sheba's famous visit to King Solomon of Israel and the coronation

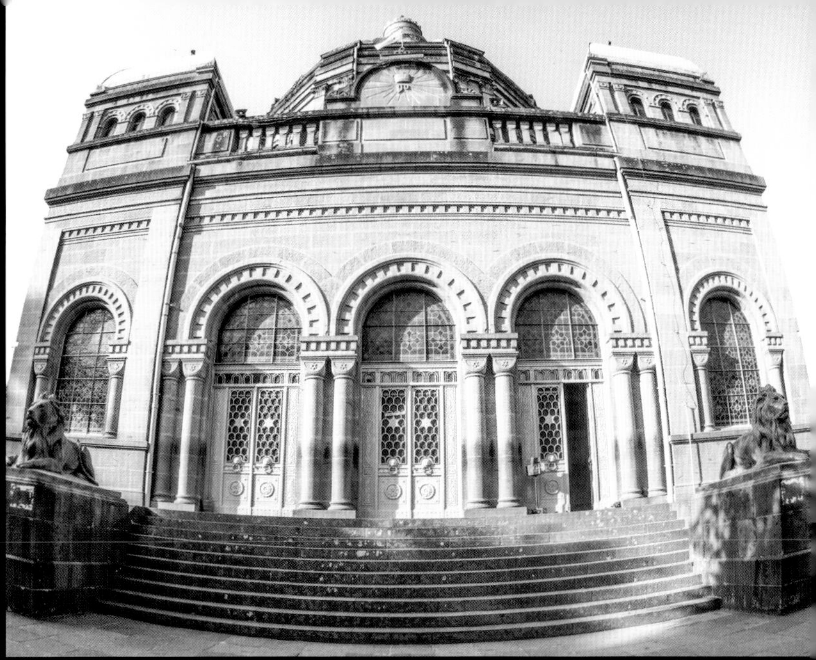

Left: Green and gold-toned throne of Emperor Menelik II and Empress Taitu. Right: A front view of the Be'ata Maryam Church shows three arched entrance doors and two arched windows guarded by lion statues. Below: Lying Christ Statue, located in the Menelik Mausoleum was a gift given to Empress Zewditu by the Greek government in 1924.

A flight of red-carpeted stairs leads to the Menelik Mausoleum, a lower chamber located underneath the nave of the church. It contains the crypts of Emperor Menelik II; his wife, Empress Taitu; and his daughter, Empress Zewditu. The remains of Princess Tsehai Haile Selassie, and those of Abba Mathias who crowned Emperor Menelik II at Entoto Maryam Church in 1890, are also found in the mausoleum

At the first take, the room overwhelms with its five tombs, various paintings, and artifacts. However a closer look at the items reveals the wealth of visual history compacted in each object. There are collections of Empress Zewditu's books alongside the traditional drums used to issue royal proclamations Other relics include the thrones of Emperor Menelik II and Empress Taitu. These thrones were carved out of a single block of wood and are attractively decorated with green fabric and gold paints.

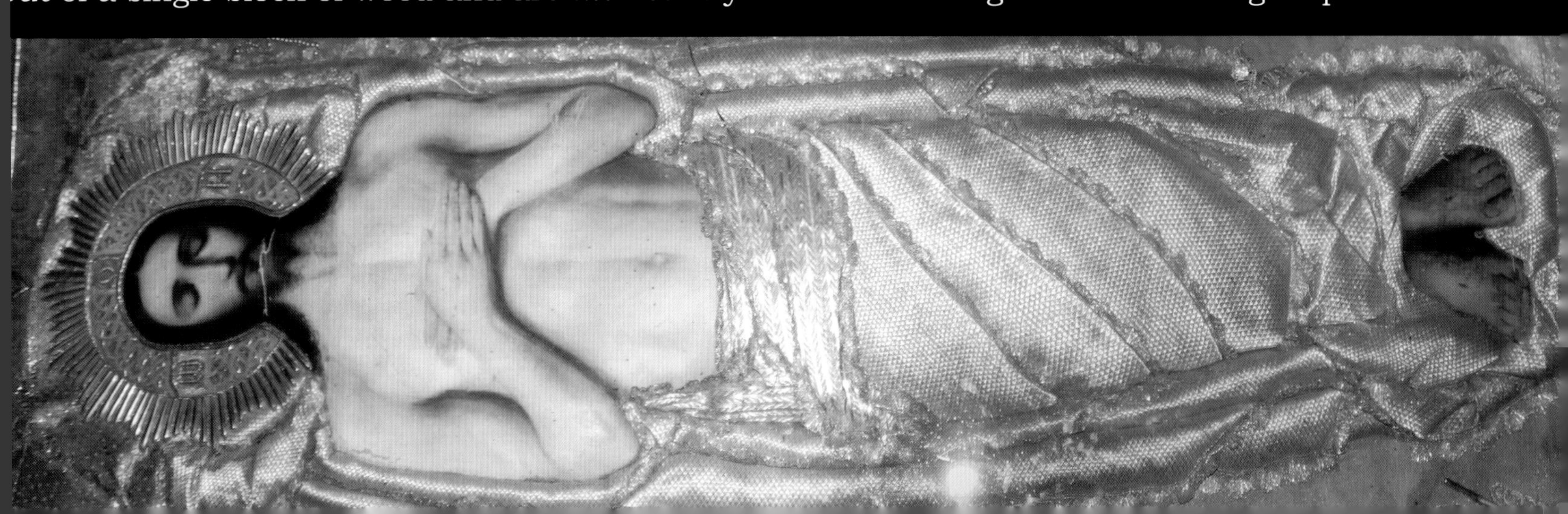

St. George Cathedral Museum

Genete Tsige Saint George Cathedral is located in the Arada sub-city, near the Addis Ababa city hall. Its establishment is closely linked to Ethiopia's victory over the Italians at the Battle of Adwa. Emperor Menelik II carried the "Tabote" of Saint George to the battlefield as the patron and savior of the nation. Upon his victorious return from the battle, the Emperor ordered the immediate construction of the church.

A Tabote is a consecrated altar slab, made of wood or stone; it symbolizes the Ark of the Covenant (containing the Ten Commandments) and represents the presence of God in every Ethiopian Orthodox Tewahedo Church.

Saint George Museum, located in Bell Tower within the compound of the church, was established in 1990. The museum's mission is to preserve artifacts that are significant in the history of Ethiopia for generations to come. Exhibits in the museum include: a photograph of the 1917 crowning of Empress Zewditu, costumes of spiritual leaders, ecclesiastical text on parchments, imperial thrones and a replica of the Saint George Tabote that the Emperor took to the Battle of Adwa

Above: The coronations of Empress Zewditu and Emperor Haile Selassie I occurred in Saint George's Cathedral. Left: A wooden cabinet display inside the Saint George Museum. Below right: Czar Nicholas II of Russia sent this bell as a souvenir to Emperor Menelik in 1896. Below left: Abune Petros (see page 29) is an Ethiopian bishop who became a martyr on July 29, 1936, during the struggle against colonialism and oppression. This original statue, located in the compound of St. George Church, shows him with full bishopric robe and holding a Bible. A new statue stands at the Abune Petros Square; it shows him with a chain and gun, highlighting the Italians' vicious treatment and Abune Petros's deep convictions

The dominant Ethiopian Orthodox Tewahedo church architectures are the circular and octagonal type with a tripartite configuration. The outer chamber of such churches is called *Qene Mahelet*, a place where the cantors sing hymns. The second chamber where the liturgical processions and Holy Communion take place is known as *Kidist*. The most sacred inner chamber is called Mekdes. This section consists of the altar on which the *Tabote*, the replica of the Ark of the Covenant, is placed.

Saint George is an octagonal Cathedral. The outer walls of the Mekdes are covered with paintings by Ethiopia's renowned artist, Afewerk Tekle. Among them are the paintings of the meeting of King Solomon and Queen of Sheba, and the 1930 coronation of Haile Selassie I as King of Kings.

The Ethiopian Tewahedo Orthodox Church Patriarchate Museum and Library is located at the Patriarchate Office near the National Museum of Ethiopia. It was established in 1996 with a mission of protecting the legacy of past spiritual leaders and preserving religious artifacts for the appreciation and edification of generations to come.

The Museum's diverse collections include vestments of Holy patriarchs, rare manuscripts and chronographically arranged photographs of past religious leaders. Other relics on display include: crowns, icons, processional crosses and patriarch crosier.

Right: Front view of Patriarchate Museum. Below: Inside the Patriarchate Museum

Richly hued paintings, depicting scenes from biblical stories, cover the walls of the museum and enlighten visitors of Ethiopia's deep connection to Christianity. A library located at the ground floor of the building enriches visitors with countless religious, cultural and historical books.

Addis Ababa has 14 public parks spread throughout the city, providing much-needed open space for recreational use. These parks offer solace from the city's growing traffic. Their significance and popularity will only increase as the city's population grows. Currently, the parks offer a perfect escape from the city's traffic and construction gridlock.

Each park is similar in its purpose while maintaining its own unique characteristics and attributes. The Bihere Tsige Flower Garden, for example, is a perfect place to visit over 6,000 varieties of flowers, shrubs, and trees. Lion Park, on the other hand, combines the tranquility of a park with the rush of getting close to lions and their cubs. The Park also houses tortoises, baboons, monkeys, rabbits, ducks, and fish.

Addis Ababa's parks are also a great place for families to spend the day as well as a perfect backdrop to those involved in romance. With permits, visitors are allowed to shoot their family and wedding photographs while maintaining other patrons' comfort.

Below: Peacock Park. Opposite page: Sheger Park

Addis Ababa Lion Park

Many scientists and researchers continue their dire warnings about the rapid decline of the lion population in Africa. A recent Duke University study estimates the number of lions now living on the savannahs to be as low as 32,000, down from nearly 100,000 in 1960. Despite these findings, Addis Ababa's Lion Zoo Park is one place visitors can experience the majestic beauty and strength of the brown hairy-maned lions. As the name of the Park implies, its major attraction is the lions, which are inside a round metal enclosure. The main enclosure is divided into eight cells designed to house couples safely, away from inquisitive visitors.

These cats are awe-inspiring, beautiful animals, they are quick to demonstrate their natural tendency as predators. Their piercing eyes and collectively loud growls are guaranteed to jolt the senses and demand complete respect.

From their symbolism of bravery to their depiction in classic and contemporary arts, Ethiopian lions have continued to possess high cultural importance. Locally, they are known by their Amharic name *Anbessa*, a term that is also bestowed on a person of heroic accomplishments and immense courage.

The Park, located near the Martyrs Memorial Square at Sidist Kilo, was established in 1984. The original residents of the zoo descended from the personal collection of Haile Selassie I, the emperor of Ethiopia from 1930 to 1974. The lions were kept at the emperor's palace, known as Genete Leul, now located within the present Addis Ababa University.

There are 15 lions currently living in the zoo. Although some have lost their mates due to old age, other couples continue to live in harmony. The illustration on right shows the names of each lion in the cell. Both the females and males are named after world-renowned Ethiopian athletes.
Worku Gemeda (M)
Tenker Geremew (M)
Mekonnen Tegatew (M)
Berkeya Tenker (F)
Gofer Worku (M)
Webnesh Chala (F)
Solomon Teka (M)
Senayet Worku (F)
Kenenesa B. Worku (M)
Meseret D. Worku (F)
Kagnew Worku (M)
Leyesh Terefe (F)
Tirunesh D. Worku (C)
Ejigayehu D. Worku (C)
Haile G. Worku (M)
(M)= Male
(F) = Female
(C) = Cube

Arts and Crafts

There was a time when everything made was a craft, functional and processed by hand. In fact, in most rural areas of Ethiopia, everyday utilitarian household goods are still made by hand, with function as the primary goal. Addis Ababa offers arts and crafts that are not only functional but also decorative. The strings of souvenir shops on Churchill Road, Merkato, and other locations in the city are examples of this fact. A first look at any handcraft and jewelry shop results in astonishment and confusion. The sheer magnitude of jewelry collections, beads, wooden sculptures, clay pots, fabric works, and other items displayed requires a few minutes of acclimatization.

The city of Addis Ababa supports the development of contemporary art by allowing artists to use part of Ferensay Park, a large urban green space near the French Embassy. The Netsa Art Village was established in 2008 by 11 graduates of Addis Ababa University's School of Fine Arts and Design. The photograph on this page shows Tesfahun Kibru's work displayed on the grounds of the Park. Ordinary pipes, car parts, and other scrap metals come together to make an artistic expression of a lady driving a car. The talented artists at the village have created other small and large projects worthy of a visitor's time.

ainting in Ethiopia dates back many centuries. he murals and paintings found throughout the ountry's historic churches convey the use of art s a communication tool to enrich spiritual depth. lthough at first art was used exclusively to communicate religious symbolism, cultural influences, echniques, and traditional methodologies were ubsequently infused to produce today's contemporary art genres.

nside the Guramayle Art Center located in Piassa, near Ras Mekonnen Bridge

Fast-forward to today. Thanks to the city's art nstitutions, galleries, and growing number of art enthusiast communities, contemporary art appreciation has continued to grow. There are now art galleries, restaurants, and cafés serving as permanent venues for both seasoned and promising artists to exhibit and sell their work to the public.

The Makush Art Gallery and Restaurant has successfully combined fine art and food to offer a unique and refreshing dining experience. One of the expressionistic paintings (shown at the top of the next column) hanging there depicts women's mportance in this world, the creativity of the young artist Elias Areda. While some artists reflect economic and social developments in their paintings, others draw their inspiration from both the world around them and their internal soul.

Elements of religion and culture are among the unique DNA distinguishing Ethiopian art from others. Anchored by a culture of several millennia, today's Ethiopia embraces both traditional and modern ways of life. This phenomenon is also apparent in the handicraft industry where functionality, aesthetics, and modernism are infused with traditional values to produce an assortment of unique Ethiopian handcrafts.

The Saint George Art Gallery (shown below) offers a fine collection of handcrafted furniture, paintings by leading Ethiopian artists, contemporary and traditional jewelry, antiques, and art objects as well as an extensive collection of fine Ethiopian silver crosses.

MODERN ART MUSEUM
GEBRE KRISTOS DESTA CENTER

ADDIS ABABA UNIVERSITY HAS DEVOTED THIS MUSEUM TO CONTRIBUTE TO THE INTELLECTUAL AND CULTURAL LIFE OF ETHIOPIA AS WELL AS TO HOST GEBRE KRISTOS DESTA'S ARTISTIC ACHIEVEMENT

THIS HISTORICAL BUILDING HAS BEEN REFURBISHED THROUGH THE SUPPORT OF THE FEDERAL REPUBLIC OF GERMANY

OCTOBER 10, 2008

Gebre Kristos Desta was one of Ethiopia's leading modern artists. A painter and poet, he received his training as an artist at the Academy of Arts in Cologne, Germany, from 1958–1961 where he became interested in abstract and expressionistic paintings (*Encyclopaedia Aethiopica: D-Ha, p.617*) In 2005, about 30 of his paintings were moved from Staatliches Museum in Munich, Germany to Addis Ababa to form a permanent exhibition at the Siddist Kilo compound of Addis Ababa University.

Above: Inside Gebre Kristos Desta center, Golgotha and other abstract painting are on display. Below: The story of Ethiopian handicrafts dates back several millennia. The sheer versatility of the various materials used to create handcrafted gift items make them truly one-of-a-kind. Religious symbols, culture, and creativity are expressed in the designs and creation of these masterpieces.

Jewelry

The beauty of pure gold is incomparable and has been used in jewelry for centuries. The Ethiopian historic connection and affection toward gold is obvious to see in the nation's museums, churches, and monasteries. The treasure in Axum, for example, contains several antique crowns made from gold and other precious stones. Some churches even continue to care for processional crosses made entirely from gold.

A stroll through Piassa, the oldest district in Addis Ababa, reveals the many gold and silver shops catering to both local and visiting customers. Located in the Gulele sub-city, Piassa offers jewelry seekers the opportunity to enjoy both innovative designs and competitive prices. Jewelry shop owners say that while the demand for imported jewelry is increasing, the popularity of local products representing religious, social, and historic messages remains strong.

Above: Assorted gold and ivory jewelry locally produced including crosses symbolizing Christianity in Ethiopia. Their elaborate, stylized designs are markedly distinct from those produced elsewhere in the world.

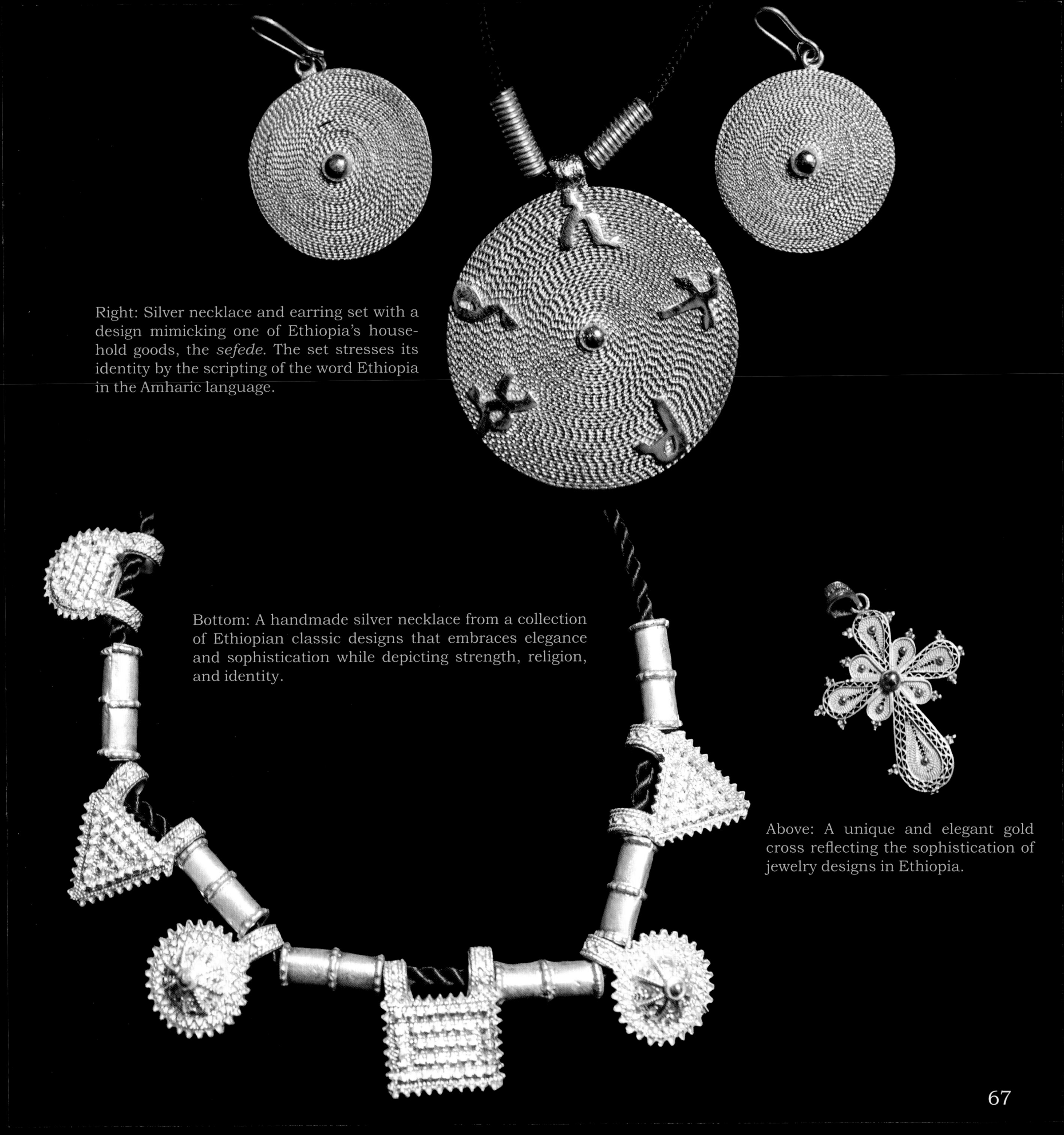

Right: Silver necklace and earring set with a design mimicking one of Ethiopia's household goods, the *sefede*. The set stresses its identity by the scripting of the word Ethiopia in the Amharic language.

Bottom: A handmade silver necklace from a collection of Ethiopian classic designs that embraces elegance and sophistication while depicting strength, religion, and identity.

Above: A unique and elegant gold cross reflecting the sophistication of jewelry designs in Ethiopia.

Traditional Dress

Addis Ababa is not only the capital of Ethiopia but also its top shopping city. Shopping for traditional clothes in Ethiopia is an experience! Around the city are boutiques displaying mannequins wearing designs of hand-woven traditional clothes. Some of the boutiques cater exclusively to Western-style clothes, while others employ creative modern interpretations of Ethiopia's classic designs. Needless to say, visitors to Addis Ababa are presented with a wide range of options for traditional and contemporary cotton products.

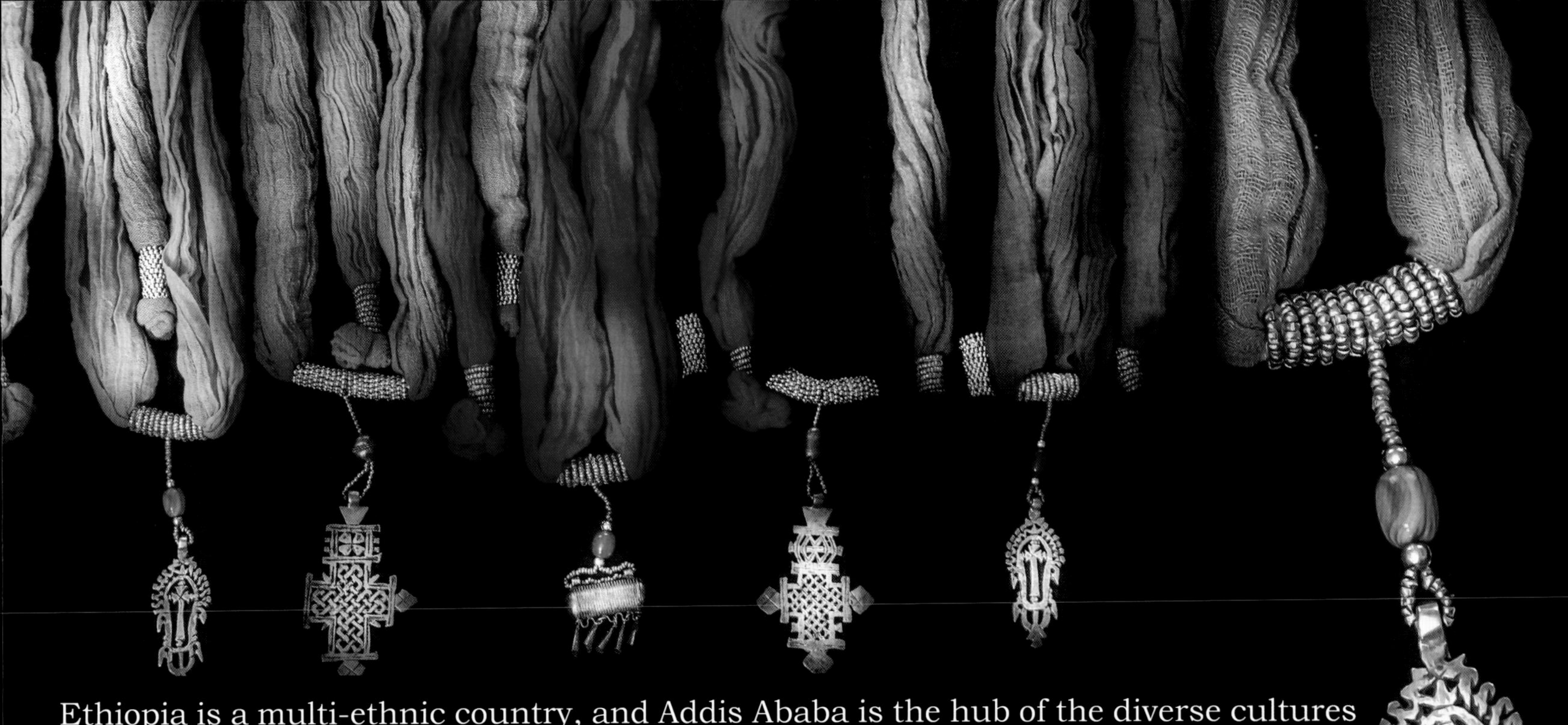

Ethiopia is a multi-ethnic country, and Addis Ababa is the hub of the diverse cultures and traditions of all ethnic groups. When the traditional cloth designs are combined with accessories and traditional hairstyles, they express an identity traceable to a geographic region within the country. Although materials used to make most traditional clothes in Ethiopia stay the same, the weaving styles and colors vary from region to region.

Today's styles transcend the classic white traditional cloth with the introduction of a wider array of colors and aesthetic appeal. Brightly colored, hand-spun cotton scarves, pillowcases, table runners, curtains, and cotton cloth napkins are dyed with natural dyes. Innovators are overhanging Ethiopian-style silver jewelry onto their designs of scarves to accessorize and enhance casual looks. A closer look at both classic and contemporary designs shows the national pride and inspiration drawn from Ethiopia's rich and diverse culture

NATIONAL THEATRE

The Ethiopian National Theatre is located on Churchill Road, a block away from the historic Ras Hotel. The theatre was completed in 1955, just in time for the celebration of the Silver Jubilee of the coronation of Emperor Haile Selassie I. Over time, it has served as a venue for live stage productions as well as local and international cinema.

The main entrance to the building leads to a grandiose marble stairs and the lobby, a perfect backdrop for the timeless pictures displayed on the walls. To the left of the main building are rooms that serve as training stages and administrative offices. To the right is an enclosed garden equipped with an outdoor restaurant and café. Although the building shows its age, the memories of Ethiopia's first-rate theatre productions, movies, and other performances make catching a play at the Ethiopian National Theatre a must when in Addis.

Left: Located in the compound of the National Theatre is a landmark sculpture of a walking man. Bottom: A view of the National Theatre auditorium.

HAGER FIKIR THEATRE

The Ethiopian Patriotic Association (Hager Fikir Maheber) was the bedrock to the foundation of the Hager Fikir Theatre. When the organization was founded in 1935, its focus was to draw resources to stand against the impending Italian invasion. After liberation in 1941, the theatre flourished and evolved into a place where creativity was born and nurtured. Today, the theatre serves as a venue for musical performances, classic plays, and modern performances.

Left: Located in the compound of the Hager Fikir Theatre, a sculpture mimicking a dynamically posed lady breathing the fresh air of art and creativity. Above: Hager Fikir Theater main entrance. Bottom: A view of the Hager Fikir Theatre auditorium.

Above: The very talented Ethiopian traditional dancer, Zinash Tsegaye dancing to Gurage traditional music.

Traditional Songs and Dance

Visiting all corners of Ethiopia is an ambitious project, requiring ample time and resources. However, attending an Ethiopian traditional music show is a pleasant way of being introduced to ethnic groups in the country. One can enjoy authentic music accompanied by traditional instruments and dances to serve as a preview of the lifestyles, cultures, and values of the people. The shows also connect with Ethiopia's long history of harmony and pride by delivering messages of unity through ethnically distinct patriotic songs

Above: The very talented Ethiopian traditional dancer, Melaku

Traditional Musical Instruments

Ethiopian musical instruments have been used for centuries in both religious ceremonies and secular entertainment. The typical instruments accompanying the religious ceremonies are the *kebero* and *sistrum.* Others, like the *begena* and *masinko* (one-stringed Ethiopian violin), frequently complement religious processions outside the church.

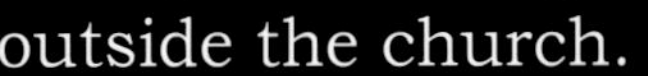

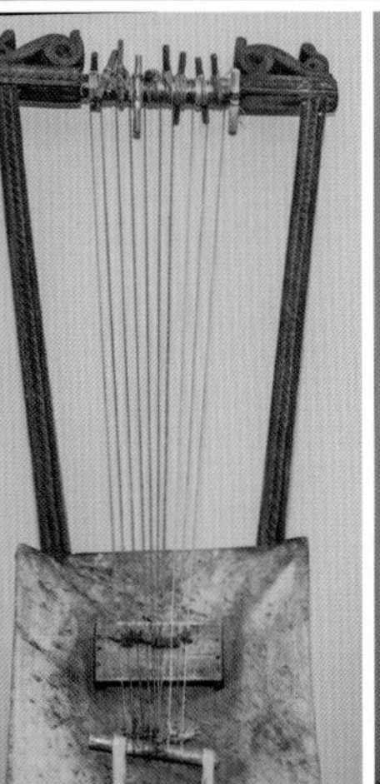

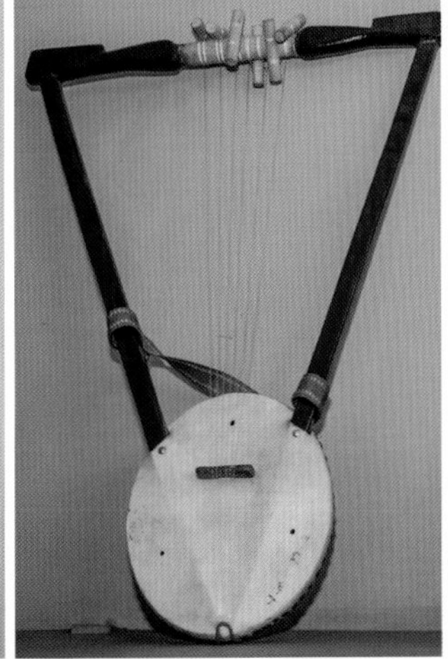

Far Left: A *begena* is a stringed instrument with 10 strings that resemble a large lyre.

Left: A *kirar* is a five- or six-stringed instrument classified in the lyre family. This instrument has been used in Ethiopia for centuries, often associated with Tizita (a blues-like genre) and love songs.

Far left: A *washint* is an Ethiopian edge-blown flute with four finger holes. The washint produces an interesting and unique sound and can be played solo as well as in an ensemble of traditional instruments. Shepherd boys often play the washint to soothe their cattle and pass time spent alone in the field. Yohannes Afework, a renowned musician is known for his superior skills of playing the washint.

Above: *Kebero*, a cylindrical, dual-sided wooden drum, beats in a spiritual context with metaphorical meaning. A large version of the instrument [shown above] is used in Orthodox Christian liturgical music as a means of celebration. A smaller version is often played in combination with other instruments in secular traditional celebrations.

A *masinko* is a single-stringed fiddle made from horsehair, with the diamond-shaped resonator covered with stretched parchment and supporting an A-shaped bridge, resembling a violin. It is played with a D-shaped bow. Right: Ethiopian Traditional Music expert and teacher, Alemayehu Fanta playing the masinko.

Sport

Long-distance running is a sport Ethiopians absolutely adore. Ever since Abebe Bikila's victory at the 1960 Olympic games in Rome and the 1964 games in Tokyo, Ethiopians' success of winning any competition has always been expected and usually achieved.

Abebe Bikila

Abebe Bikila was the first African to win an Olympic gold medal. He won the marathon running barefoot in Rome in 1960 and won again wearing shoes in Tokyo in 1964, becoming the first person to win the most grueling of all human contests twice.

Abebe Bikila was laid to rest on the grounds of Saint Joseph's Church in Addis Ababa on October 25, 1973. In his honor, a statue of him stands in Saint Joseph's Cemetery.

Soccer is the most widespread sport in Ethiopia. The national team's 2013 qualification to the African Cup of Nations invigorated the sport to levels unseen in recent memory. Spectators of the sport are die-hard fans of their favorite teams. The allegiance to soccer goes beyond the country's borders to the European professional league competitions.

Opposite page: Abebe Bikila's statue at his burial site. Above: The Ethiopian national football team at a qualifier game in Addis Ababa. Below left: The Great Run, annual 10-kilometre road running event that takes place in late November in Addis Ababa. Below right: Diehard fans wearing the national team's jersey.

Transportation

According to a Ministry of Transportation's policy report, there is a big gap between public transportation demand and supply. The claim is supported by the daily rush hour chaos playing out on the streets of Addis. The 500 Anbessa busses, 50 Higer busses, the 9,000 minibus taxis and thousands of aged Saloon taxis are no match for the city's expanding geographical area and growing population.

The Light Rail Transit

The construction of the Light Rail Transit (LRT) system is one solution the city has heavily invested in to improve the overburdened transportation network. When completed, the LRT promises to provide convenient transit services, connecting thousands of the city's residents to major business districts, as well as medical, educational, and entertainment centers.

Top left and right: Few of the first cars in Addis Ababa. Above Workers laying rail track for the light rail transit system.

Early February 2015 marked the official launch of trial runs of the Addis Ababa Light Railway trains. When fully implemented, the project is expected to alleviate the city's growing transportation problems.

Ethiopian Airlines

Ethiopian Airlines was founded in December 1945. A flag carrier of Ethiopia, the airline has become one of Africa's leading carriers. With a fleet of more than 77 airplanes, the airline provides ample service to many international and domestic destinations. The non-stop service to Asia, Europe, and North America added to its prestige while promoting its stance as a gateway to Africa. The only one of its kind in the country, Ethiopian Airlines is also at the forefront of self-sufficiency in aviation-related training. Its Aviation Academy division offers training for pilots, technicians, cabin crew, and supporting staff. In mid-2012, Ethiopia, through Ethiopian Airlines, became the second country after Japan to take delivery of the Boeing 787 Dreamliner.

Bole International Airport

The Addis Ababa Bole International Airport, located only eight kilometers from the city center, is the hub for Ethiopian Airlines. In addition to the international terminal, the airport has an enclave dedicated to domestic flights. The newer, modern airport terminal was inaugurated on January 21, 2003.

he Nations, Nationalities, and Peoples' Square, also known as the Gotera interchange, connects fou
f the city's busy roads catering to hundreds of vehicles throughout the day. The multi-deck inter-
hange accommodates cars, light railways, and walking traffic in all four directions of the city. Prior to
ompletion, the interchange was nicknamed the Confusion Square because of its counterintuitive path
nd frequent traffic congestion.

Religion

The harmonious existence between Christianity and Islam i
Ethiopia dates back centuries. Addis Ababa's skyline is a prim
example of such cohesiveness and respect among people of differen
faiths. In the metropolitan area alone, there exist over 125 Orthodo
Christian churches and over 145 mosques. Addis Ababa resident
have enough awareness of each other's holidays and landmarks t
appreciate and tolerate their differences. The personal virtue exem
plified by the Ethiopian people is demonstrated by the respect an
appreciation for each other's religion, ultimately promoting a col
lective strength as one people.

Below: Inside Medhanialem Church near Bole International Airport. Left: Ethiopia prayer stick. Opposite page: Side view of the Medhanialem Church

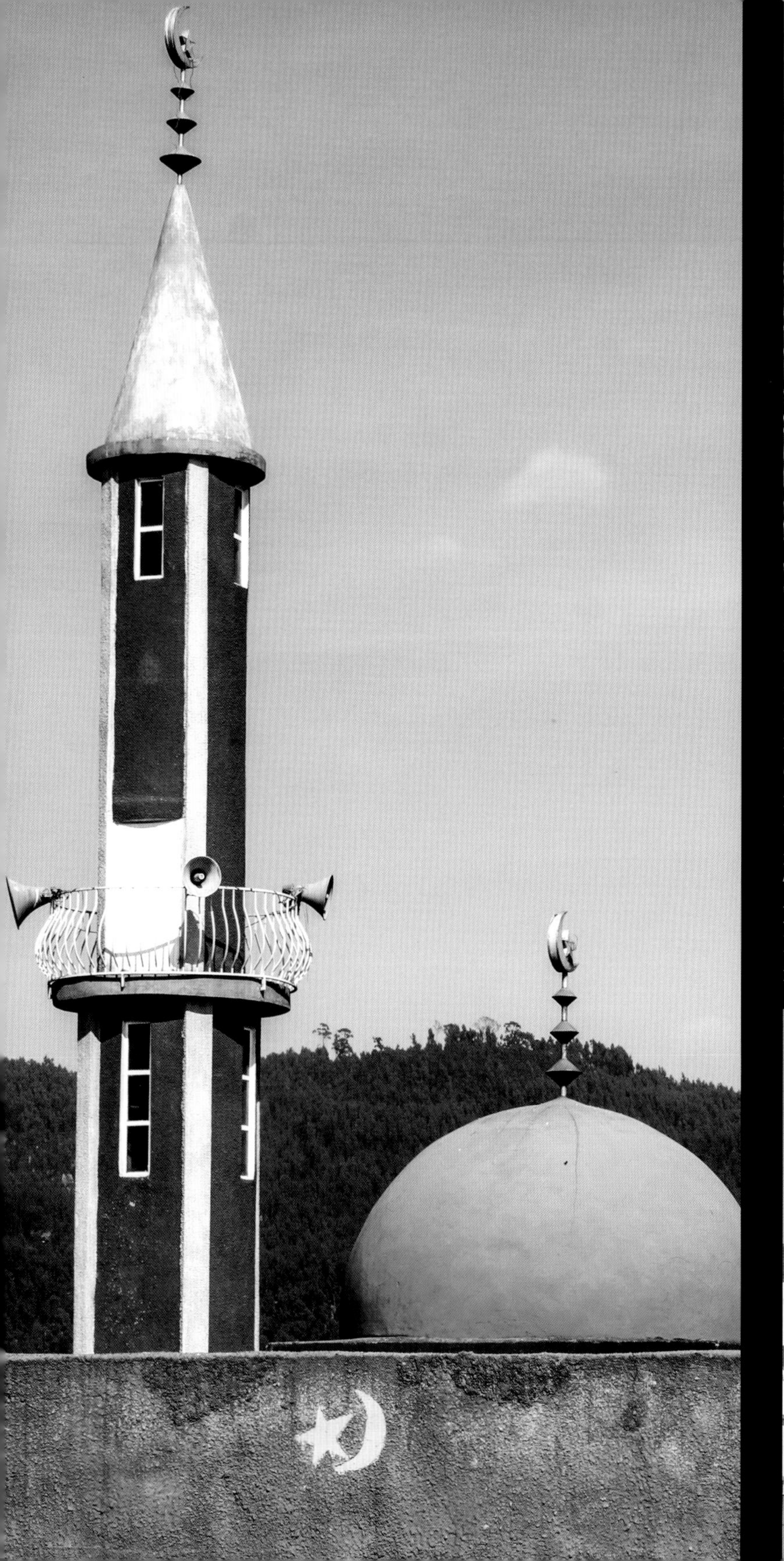

Opposite page: Every Friday at noon, Muslims go to a Mosque for a gathering or Jumaa prayer. The picture shows the Jumaa at the Al-Noor Mosque in the Piassa area, uniquely identified as Benine. Above: Eid al-Fitr is an Islamic festival celebration denoting the end of the Ramadan fasting season. In Addis Ababa, the celebration often takes place in the city's main square to accommodate the growing number of pilgrims. Left: Wele Mohammed the first mosque in Addis Ababa, located in the Yeka sub-city near the Menelik Palace. The Mosque was built in 1898. Below: The largest mosque in Addis Ababa, the Al-Anwar Mosque (also known as The Grand Anwar Mosque) was built in 1922. The Mosque is located in Merkato near Ethiopia's largest open-air market.

Festivals

The Ethiopian calendar marks religious feasts, fasts, and holidays that are observed throughout the year. As an integral part of Ethiopian life and culture, the religious festivals are celebrated with inspiring ceremonies, vibrant colors and spiritual music.

GENNA - Christmas | January 7

In the Gregorian calendar, Christmas is observed on the 25th of December. Since Ethiopia follows the ancient Julian calendar, Christmas falls and is celebrated on January 7. Festive activities include attending early morning church service and playing a traditional hockey-like game named after the holiday. Genna is also a holiday when people dress up and visit relatives.

Meskel - Easter | Sept. 24

Meskel is a holiday celebrated by the Ethiopian Orthodox Christians commemorating the discovery of the True Cross upon which Jesus was crucified. To symbolize Queen Helena's (Mother of Roman Emperor Constantine) burning of incense and praying for help in guidance to the location of the True Cross, tall branches are tied together and ignited while followers gleefully pray and dance for joy around the bonfire.

TIMKET - Epiphany | January 19

Timket (baptism/Epiphany) in Ethiopia is the that celebrates the baptism of the Lord Jesus Christ in the Jordan River. Priests from all parish churches carry the Tabot (sacred replica of the Ark of the Covenant), form processions, and proceed to a nearby designated stream. Timket is celebrated on Tirr 10 of the Ethiopian calendar, January 19 (20 on leap year) on the Gregorian calendar.

Eid al-Fitr - October

Eid al-Fitr, the Festival of Breaking the Fast, comes at the end of Ramadan, a month of blessings marked by prayer, fasting, and charity. During Eid al-Fitr people dress in their finest, adorn their homes with lights and decorations, give treats to children, and enjoy visits with friends and family.

Mawlid al-Nabi - April

This holiday celebrates the birthday of the Prophet Mohammed, the founder of the Islam religion. It is fixed as the 12th day of the month of Rabi on the Islamic calendar. Followers of Islam observe the holiday by going to Mosques and attending the communal prayer. The celebration continues at home by feasting with family and friends.

FASIKA - Easter | April 20

Fasika is one of the holidays on the Ethiopian calendar; it commemorates the resurrection of Christ. The holiday is proceeded by a Holy Lent fast lasting 55 and culminating on Easter Sunday. The end of the feast is celebrated in colorful church ceremonies often illuminated by lit candles, reverence, and joy.

Enkutatash - New Year | Sept. 11

Enkutatash is a day of celebration marking the first day of a new year. Meskerem first on the Ethiopian calendar falls on September 11 (September 12 during a leap year) on the Gregorian calendar. Although Enkutatash is observed as one of the major holidays by Orthodox Christians, it is also a day to exchange New Year greetings and good wishes. On this day, it is customary for children to present yellow daisies to relatives and neighbors.

SKYLINE

The skyline of Addis Ababa offers one-of-a-kind, thrilling, and unobstructed views of the city. Pictures taken from high grounds and rooftops highlight the city's appeal through nature's alignment with the life around it. The pictures shown on this page were taken from a construction site near Legehar and shows the contrast created by a clear sky: Mount Entoto's eucalyptus forest, modern buildings, a stadium, and the city's famous taxi commotion.

Above: The picture was taken from the grounds of Addis View, a restaurant located at the foothills of the Yeka hills. A grid filter was applied to sensationalize and highlight the city's active spots. Below: The African Union headquarters, dominates the skyline around it.

EDUCATION

Addis Ababa University was formed in 1950, making it the oldest higher education institution in Ethiopia. The school was initially named the University College of Addis Ababa (UCAA). In the early 1960s, other colleges were merged with UCAA to form Haile Selassie I University. After the 1974 revolution, the university was once again renamed to its current name, Addis Ababa University.

Today, the university has grown from its modest beginnings with a capacity of 33 students to a countrywide institution with over 48,000 students in 70 undergraduate and 293 graduate programs. It is also the home of the Institute of Ethiopian Studies and the Ethnographic Museum.

The following is an excerpt from Emperor Haile Selassie's speech during the laying of the cornerstone of the proposed new university on November 2, 1949.

"By what means can man's achievements in this world be best remembered? Many people believe that this could be done by the erection of physical and material structures; others believe that their works are in themselves lasting monuments. We, for our part, think that man's contributions which live to influence the life and progress of posterity are the most permanent monuments that can ever erect."

The water fountain in the courtyard of the Sidist Kilo campus of Addis Ababa University is commonly known among students as the Kissing Pool, signifying its popularity as a meeting place. Below: Addis Ababa University, Institute of Ethiopian Studies. Opposite page: Addis Ababa University's main gate.

አዲስ፡አበባ፡
ዩኒቨርስቲ።
ADDIS AB
UNIVERS

Yared School of Music is the first higher institution of music in Ethiopia. It was founded in 1954 by the then Ministry of Education and Fine Arts. Its former name, the National School of Music, was officially changed to Yared School of Music in 1969. A number of governmental bodies administered the school until 1999, when Addis Ababa University took over the administration and upgraded its program to a Bachelor of Arts degree level. The ultimate goal of the music departments is to increase the number of skilled professionals that meet the needs of the country in the area of music and related trades.

The school is named after Saint Yared, a legendary Ethiopian musician. He is credited with inventing the sacred music tradition of the Ethiopian Orthodox Church and Ethiopia's system of music. The statue of Saint Yared (shown to the right) is located at the lobby of the main building at the Yared School of Music compound.

Alle School of Fine Arts and Design

Mr. Alle Felege-Selam founded the Alle School of Fine Arts and Design in 1958. For many decades, the school had been the only school of its kind in Ethiopia where talented students were trained to become professional artists and art teachers. The curriculum was limited to the basics of drawing, painting, sculpture, commercial art and art education. In 1975, major program changes were made, especially in the curriculum, to include specialization in graphic arts.

The most significant change, however, occurred in 1998 when the School was united with the Addis Ababa University. Subsequently in the year 2000, degree programs were offered in Painting, Sculpture, Print-making, Industrial Design and Art Education. In 2010, The College of Performing and Visual Arts was formed comprising the School of Theatre Arts, the Yared School of Music and the School of fine Arts and Design, the Cultural Center and Modern Art Museum, Gebre-Kirestos Desta Center.

Above: The Alle School of Art has collections of fine sculptures scattered in its garden. The permanent collection includes masterpieces by past and current students and professors.

Right: Students are required to submit a final art product before they graduate. As a result, the school has a collection of paintings going back to decades.

Left: The main gallery at the Alle School of Fine Arts and Design

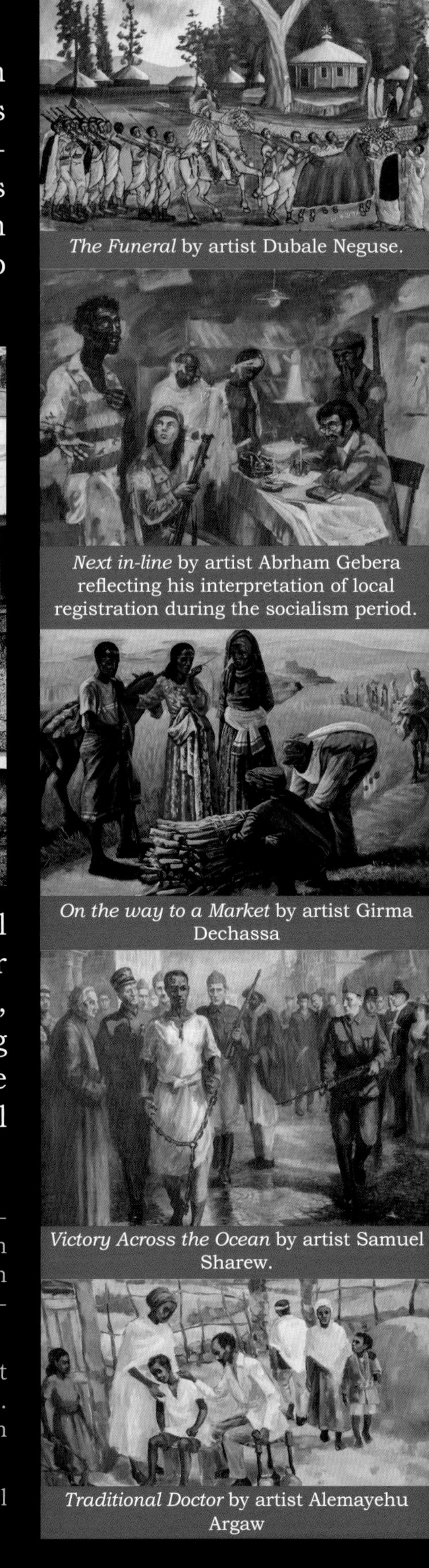

The Funeral by artist Dubale Neguse.

Next in-line by artist Abrham Gebera reflecting his interpretation of local registration during the socialism period.

On the way to a Market by artist Girma Dechassa

Victory Across the Ocean by artist Samuel Sharew.

Traditional Doctor by artist Alemayehu Argaw

CURRENCY

Ethiopia's currency is the *birr*. The present denominations of the birr in circulation are 1, 5, 10, 50, and 100. The notes (shown on the opposite page) vary in color, making their values easily identifiable. The coins are known as *santeem*; their denominations are 1 birr, 50, 25, 10, 5, and 1 cents. The photograph shows an assortment of currently used Ethiopian bills and coins, as well as a few used during the periods of Emperors Menelik II and Haile Selassie I.

Payable to the bearer on demand
TEN BIRR
ONE ETHIOPIAN DOLLAR
PAYABLE TO THE BEARER ON DEMAND
National Bank of Ethiopia
AX9112315
FIFTY BIRR
50
National Bank of Ethiopia
3898584
Payable to the bearer on demand
ONE BIRR
2000
2008
GOVERNOR
IG3898584
BANK OF ETHIOPIA
17856
ADDIS ABABA
1 Mai 1932
POUR
BANK OF ETHIOPIA
STATE BANK
ETHIOPIAN
A022995
ONE HUNDRED
ETHIOPIAN DOLLARS
PAYABLE TO THE BEARER ON DEMAND
100

Strolling around the streets of Addis is a joy. In addition to the chance to discover hidden corners and treasures, one becomes acquainted with the city's deeply rooted characteristics. Piassa, for example, exhibits distinct architecture denoting the brief occupation by the Italians. While walking in area known as Bole, gives the feeling of a bustling entertainment center within a hidden oasis.

Above: The National Bank of Ethiopia is located on Churchill Road. The circular building is a great architectural landmark. Below: The garden of the Ethiopian National Theatre is often filled with patrons who enjoy the shade while consuming food from the outdoor cafés.

Above: A picture showing one of the city's old buildings that trace back to the early 1940s. The building is also home to Castelli, one of the city's long-standing and prestigious Italian restaurants.

Piassa is a unique area with its own personality. As the name indicates, the Italians who occupied the country played a role in influencing its character. The winding streets of Piazzo are filled with jewelry shops, bookstores and cafes.

Above left: The view of Saint Raguel Ethiopian Orthodox Tewahedo Church in Merkato includes parishioners and vendors displaying church articles. Above right: Olympia is one of the main arteries into the Bole business district. Below: An early afternoon view of the Bole area commonly referred to as Bole Medhanialem. Its close proximity to the Bole International Airport, hotels, and shops gives it an energy boom distinct to the area.

TRADITIONAL FOOD

Ethiopia's food is an extension of its people's identity. Teff, spice, and butter are the staple ingredients that give Ethiopian food its strong and distinctive flavor. Teff, one of the smallest grains in the world, is used to make a spongy flatbread called *injera*. The foundation of every traditional meal, *injera* is spread across a large communal platter to be used as the bedrock for a variety of stews (wats). An assortment of vegetarian and meat wats are then carefully placed over the top of the *injera* in a colorful display.

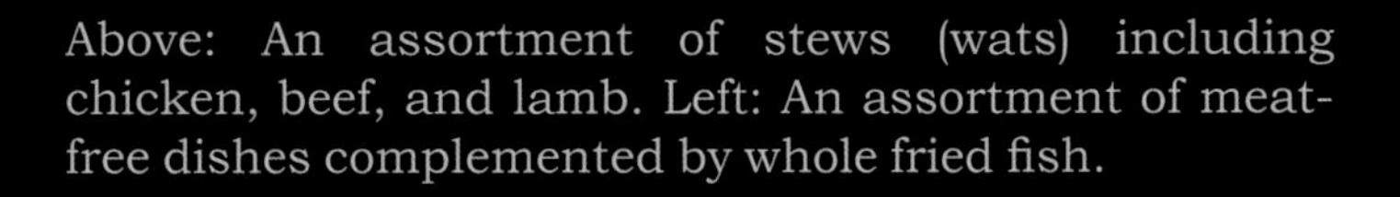

Above: An assortment of stews (wats) including chicken, beef, and lamb. Left: An assortment of meat-free dishes complemented by whole fried fish.

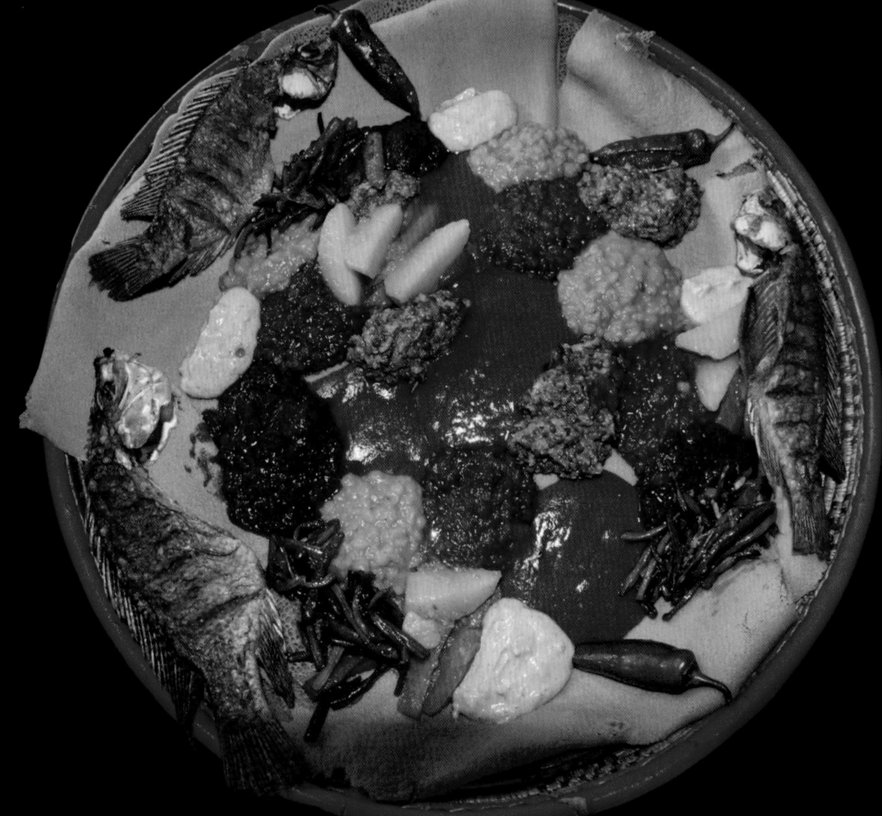

Ethiopians' culinary use of spices dates back to ancient times. To understand Ethiopian cuisine, one must appreciate the spices used in its preparation. Key wat (red stew), featuring chicken, beef, lamb, lentils, or vegetables, inherits its basic character from *berbere*, a combination of peppers, herbs, and know-how.

Entering Chane Restorant's purple metal doors to the main dining area is an act that unwraps the owner's generous, compassionate and delightful utopian dream. Mr. Chane is a man who overcame massive social, financial and ideological obstacles to realize his aspiration of becoming a chef. He serves the community with fairly priced, tasty, health conscious recipes that were passed down from generations.

When talking about his 35 years of service in the Kazanchis area, Mr. Chane's passion brings a bright glow to his face. He learned the art of cooking Ethiopian traditional food from his grand-parents. Trying to fulfill society's expectation of gender roles, Chane tried such "masculine" jobs as being a solder and a mechanic. However, his childhood exposure and love for cooking continued to pull him back to cooking. Since then he has been serving his loyal customers with epicurean delights fit for a king. In fact, the popular dishes on his menu are named after Emperor Menelik II and Empress Taitu.

His establishment is a unique place that connects today's customers to the royal recipes of the past. Every day from 12:30 to 1:45 PM, generous portions of freshly made food are combined with great friendly service and lively atmosphere to create an

In Addis Ababa, socializing around fresh and locally brewed draft beer and wine is second only to the culture of coffee. During happy hours, bars and restaurants are filled with weary professionals sipping their favorite draft beer and passionately discussing the day's events.

There are also several bottled beers sold in Addis Ababa. The sweet and consistent flavor of Saint George beer, product of the first brewery in Ethiopia, traces its beginnings back to the early 1920s. Walia, Meta, Castel, Bedele, Zemen, and Dashen are some of the other bottled beers enjoyed throughout the city.

Left: A skilled waitress holding ten Saint George full-draft glasses. Middle: Tej, Ethiopian honey wine, served in a narrow-necked glass decanter. Right: Walia, Ethiopia's newest draft beer.

The basic art of brewing homemade beer, known locally as *tella*, has been practiced in Ethiopia's households for many years. *Tella* can be made from barley, corn, or wheat. The quality of the grain and family secrets also influence the beer's character, to give each brewer's product its own individual appeal.

Tej, Ethiopian honey wine, is another home-brewed beverage served in Ethiopian homes for centuries. It is easily distinguished by its golden color, spicy sweetness, and potency. It is usually served in distinctive narrow-necked glass decanters kno

Above: Jebena, a traditional clay coffee pot. Right: Selam Kasaun, roasting coffee beans.

The Art of Coffee

Ethiopia is the birthplace of coffee. For many, drinking coffee is an entrenched routine in their daily lives. Ethiopians' love affair with coffee is illustrated by a distinctive welcoming ceremony. The ceremony starts by roasting the green coffee beans over an open-air brazier before grinding them with a wooden mortar and pestle. A *jebena*, a traditional Ethiopian coffee pot, is then used to brew the coffee to perfection. The brewing process starts by warming up water in the coffeepot. Just the right amount of coffee is then added, and the mixture is allowed to boil slowly. The experienced brewer times the procedure and uses a skillful touch to make sure the grounds are settled before the precious brew is served in demitasse cups.

bove: Inside Tomoca, the first coffee company based in Addis baba.

THE ORIGIN OF COFFEE

t is widely believed that coffee growing and lrinking began in the Horn of Africa, where, ccording to legend, coffee trees originated in Kefa, Ethiopia. In fact, the word coffee is believed o be derived from *Kefa*, the name of a coffee-rich egion in southwestern Ethiopia.

A growing number of coffee houses and restaurants in Addis Ababa serve sweet delicacies. Most dessert treats are European-inspired cakes and pastries that get paired with Ethiopia's delicious coffee and tea drinks.

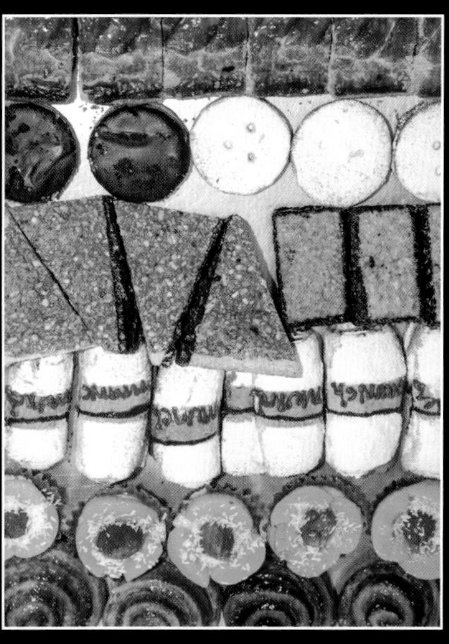

Above left: Assorted gourmet pastries from Munch, a German bakery found in three locations in the city - Bole, Old-Airpor and Kazanchis. Above right: Baklava, a signature at the Ras Mekonnen Café in Piassa, is a sweet pastry made of filo held together by a generous amount of honey. Below: Coffee roasting in an open-air brazier

A Sip of Macchiato

Macchiato is a name used by Italian baristas to differentiate a naked espresso from one with a tiny bit of milk. When in Addis, one can quickly find the drink, supplemented by Ethiopia's hospitality and friendship. In addition to the traditional coffeehouses, the city is dotted with many modern cafés and restaurants full of patrons chatting with friends and reading newspapers while sipping their choice of coffee products. Baristas, such as Wendemu at Cupcake Café, are experts at enhancing the experience with the allure of creative drawings, like the ones shown on the opposite page.

Fruit Juice

The climate and wide range of soil types in Ethiopia result in a year-round, constant flow of fresh fruits. Most Addis Ababa restaurants and cafés use avocado, banana, mango, strawberry, guava, and papaya to create appealing and tasty fruit juice blends.

Addis
ABeBA
CUP

View from Mount Entoto

Entoto is a mountain located immediately north of Addis Ababa. With an altitude of over 3,000 meters, it offers some of the most captivating views of the city. This is what makes Entoto Mountain special, combined with the crisp and fresh air, and the real sense it evokes of standing where Addis Ababa was born.

Mount Entoto is much more than just a highland covered with eucalyptus trees. There are the historic Saint Mary of Entoto Ethiopian Orthodox Church, where Menelik II was crowned emperor of Ethiopia in November 1889, his imperial compound, and the opportunities it offers for an unforgettable panoramic view of the city.

Within walking distance from Saint Mary's Church is the Entoto Museum where visitors are instructed by many artifacts that give life to Ethiopia's history. The Negarit, the drum used to announce the declaration of the Adwa War, is one of the many impressive relics displayed.

The majestic mountain is also a training ground for Ethiopia's world-renowned athletes. The challenge of Mount Entoto's highland terrain gives long-distance runners a great advantage in performance and endurance. As attested by marathon coach Dr. Yilma Berta, training on Mount Entoto is like running in heaven.

AFRICAN UNION AND ECA

Addis Ababa is home to the African Union [AU], Africa's highly prestigious organization. As the successor to the Organization of African Unity [OAU], the AU is focused on good government, democracy, rule of law, and social progress within the continent. The AU's relatively new headquarters in Addis Ababa is a sign of the organization's commitment to continue using the city as its permanent setting to discuss Africa's affairs.

Above: African Union Summit in Addis Ababa. Below: ECA Headquarters

Above: African Union Conference Center (AUCC), Addis Ababa, Ethiopia.

Addis Ababa is also home to the United Nations Economic Commission for Africa (ECA) headquarters. Established by the Economic and Social Council (ECOSOC) of the United Nations (UN) in 1958, ECA's mandate is to promote the economic and social development of its member states, to foster intraregional integration, and to promote international cooperation for Africa's development.

bove: Hilton Hotel. Below: Radisson Blu, relatively new hotel.

Hotels

Addis Ababa is the melting pot for the culturally diverse population of Ethiopia. Since the city is also Africa's choice for the African Union headquarters, it is home to a large number of international organizations. Therefore, the skyline o the city is dotted by both legendary and contemporary hotels and restaurants. Most are located a few minutes drive from each other and offer luxurious modern rooms, superb restaurants, and paramount services.

Sheraton Addis

The Sheraton Addis, located in the center of Addis Ababa, is considered one of the most luxurious hotels with amenities and services to match. Among its many features, the hotel offers a complimentary and refreshing show of water, music, and light attractively combined to mesmerize its visitors. The weekly nighttime water spectacular illuminates the hotel's manicured landscape of vibrant greens and colorful flowers.

Merkato

Merkato is not just one of the largest open-air markets in Africa; it is also an important landmark in Addis Ababa. Although the ongoing city modernization is transforming some areas of the market with buildings and shopping complexes, the current landscape still shows visitors the original bursting energy and vibrant nature of Merkato.

When visiting Merkato, one must understand the grid system, where items are grouped by type. Terra (loosely translated as section) is a key word to know for navigating the various segments. M*enalesh Terra* may be one of the most fascinating of all the sections. Since the items found in this section can't be categorized as any one type, sellers often wait until the consumer identifies what he or she is looking for. As a result, merchants are likely to ask, "What do you need?" In order to identify and make a successful sale. As one of the major attractions in the city, Merkato (shown on the opposite page) features a wide variety of products. Simply put, it is where one will find just about anything the heart desires.

Open-air Grocery

In addition to large markets, many people in Addis Ababa also buy food from open-air markets. These markets are conveniently located in neighborhoods and busy business districts. The fresh produce, out front and stacked, is an eye-catching attraction meant to appeal to consumers. Shop owners and attendants demonstrate a neighborly feel with such individualized services as taking orders and delivering to busy customers parked in the lot.

Below: Abdi Negash Hassen is Piassa's well-recognized and passionate collector of books, newspapers and other Ethiopian historical artifact. His street book kiosk and back-room are filled with relics from Ethiopia's past.

Street booksellers

Street bookstores (shown on the left) are one of Addis Ababa's treasures. Books are stacked from floor to ceiling and somewhat organized into various topical areas. Enthusiastic and casual readers find used, rare, out of print, and collectable books in all categories pertaining to Ethiopian history, culture, and more. A visitor overwhelmed by the collection —and most visitors are— can mention an interest to the friendly seller, who will assist in finding something to satisfy.

Shoe-shine boys

The shoeshine boys in Addis Ababa play an important role in the city's collective dynamic. The occupation is historically known as the starting point for many boys who have used the hard work, business agility, and knowledge gained as the stepping-stone to a successful future.

Egg quality inspection

Experienced farmers in Ethiopia use the age-old visual method of inspection to identify spoiled eggs. In addition to the obvious, they are able to use bright sunlight to examine inside the shells to discover which eggs are unusable.

Street performers

It is not unusual to find talented street performers in Addis Ababa. Ethiopian solo minstrels, known locally as *azmari*, help brighten the days with tunes and lyrics, often customized to their audience's appearance and generosity.

Chat

Chat is a mildly narcotic plant that has been chewed for years. Usually accompanied by glasses of tea or soft drinks, chat is known to cause excitement, loss of appetite, and euphoria. It is common in Addis Ababa to see chat sellers carrying bundles of twigs, stems, and leaves wrapped in banana leaves.

CITY VIBES

EGG QUALITY INSPECTION

SHOE-SHINE BOYS

CHAT

STREET PERFORMERS

Nightlife

Nightlife in Addis Ababa is limited only by the energy level and interests of its visitors. From lavish lounges with the ultimate stylish experience to friendly cultural bars, the city extends its unparalleled social and cultural experiences.

Many upscale bars and lounges have in-house DJs who play contemporary Ethiopian, American, and other popular music on excellent quality sound systems. Some modern dance clubs, such as Gaslight at the Sheraton, further enhance the experience with state-of-the-art dance floor lighting and laser shows.

If clubs are not the entertainment of choice traditional restaurants offer music from all corners of the country. While promoting Ethiopia's cultures, places like *Checheho* Traditional Restaurant introduce visitors to a range of cultural cuisines and a variety of tribal songs and dances.

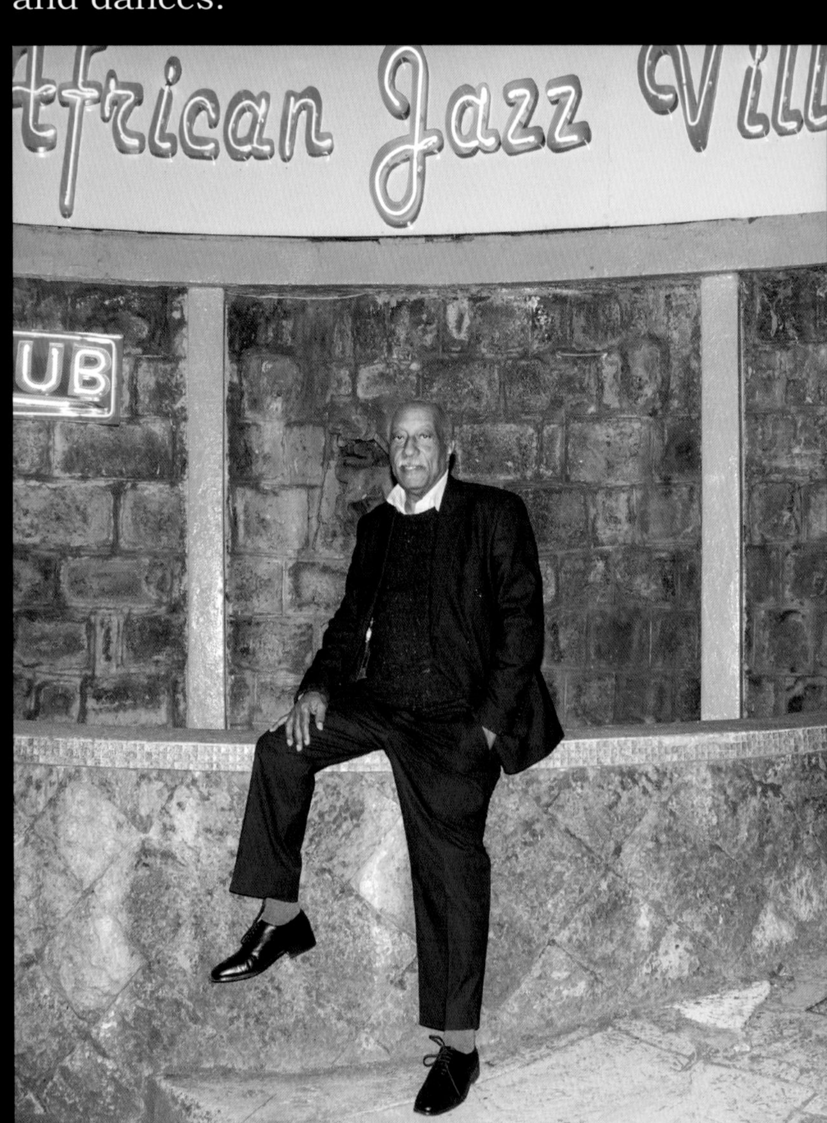

The launch of African Jazz Village brings the chance of spending your evening listening to the world-renowned father of Ethio-jazz, Mulatu Astatke. The club is located inside the historical Ghion Hotel, near the football stadium.

Azmari Bet (the House of Azmari) is where people go to listen to and enjoy traditional music. An azmari is a multi-talented artist with the skills of playing the masinko and carrying a tune. Their humorous perspective and impromptu delivery make them great entertainers. Fendika Azmari Bet, located in Kazanchis, uniquely combines azmari music with professional musicians, dancers, and singers.

A perfect early beginning is the jumping-off point to a great night out. When the late afternoon rush hour settles, Addis Ababa transforms into a calmer serene phase. Cafés serving Ethiopia's famous coffee and fruit juices are great places to fill the gap while waiting for the nightlife to start. If longer breaks are required, the city offers the latest and greatest flicks that will compete for attention at one of the many movie theatres around the city. The rapidly growing Ethiopian motion picture industry is producing low-budget, quality movies ranging from romance and drama to comedy.

Other options include passing time with friends and family while enjoying early night piano and jazz sessions. Samuel Yirga (shown above) is a young Ethiopian musician and composer signed to the world music label, Real World Records. Visitors get a chance to see him perform in one of the many clubs in Addis. Every Thursday, the Four Start Band (shown below) plays smooth jazz and Ethiopian oldies for a mature crowd. They can be seen from 7 to 9:30 PM at Jupiter Hotel in Kazanchis.

If one's travel schedule allows a day trip, a surprising number of great breaks can be found just beyond the city's periphery. Breathtaking lakes, beautiful scenery, and naturally attractive vacation destinations are a few of the many delights that compete to capture one's attention. Opposite Page: The lime-green water of Lake Bishoftu seen from Dreamland Family Resort.

Ensessakotteh is a wildlife rescue conservation and education center located 30 kilometers from Addis Ababa. The center is managed by Born Free Foundation of Ethiopia, which collaborates with the Ethiopian Wildlife Conservation Authority (EWCA). Ensessakotteh is not a zoo. Its aim is to provide rehabilitation facilities for wild animals seized from illegal trade, found orphaned or injured. Those that cannot be released to the wild are provided with care for life at the center.

Ensessakotteh offers an escape, a peaceful haven for visitors who can enjoy the beautiful surroundings that retain much of the wild fauna and flora. However, the organization's primary goal is to rescue and care for animals; therefore the number of visitors to the center is limited. The staff recommends would-be visitors call before commencing to drive.

Lake Langano

Lake Langano is located 200 kilometers south of the capital. The brown-water lake is a perfect place for boating, swimming, or simply basking in the sun.

Wondo Genet

Above: The Wondo Genet hot springs are located 260 kilometers south of Addis Ababa. Wondo Genet's dense forest and ho springs combination offers visitors and bird life enthusiasts a balanced setting.

Sodere

Above: Sodere is a spa town located 125 kilometers southeast of Addis Ababa. The area is known foremost for its hot springs and resort hotels.

LAKE ZIWAY

A few hours drive from Addis Ababa is the city of Ziway and Lake Ziway. The lake is known for its scenic quality and dense bird population.

Among the many Ethiopian Orthodox monasteries in and around Addis Ababa, Debre Libanos is the largest. It is like a mini-city and is home to hundreds of monks, nuns, and hermits. There, the simplicity and devotion exemplified by monastic life are on display. Only 130 kilometers from the city center, the landscape and scenic atmosphere are an idyllic backdrop to the flourishing life of the monks.

Tekle-Haymanot was an indigenous Ethiopian monk who founded the Debre Libanos monastery. He is also one of the revered saints of the Ethiopian Orthodox Tewahedo Church, recognized amongst Ethiopians and followers of Orthodox Christianity outside the country. The painting to the right is located at the entrance of a cave where the saint lived in the nearby cliffs. It depicts the legend of the winged Saint Tekle-Haymanot praying for seven years while standing on one leg.

Monastic Life

The Ethiopian Orthodox monastic life requires nothing short of complete dedication to the ways of Christian being. A monk is expected to ground her life and conduct in Christ. She rises early and separates herself from others to pray for the sins of the world.

Monks in Debre Libanos are the first to say that they aren't perfect. Most of them emphasize one claim; they try to ignore the worldly life to pursue one based on the teachings of God. They also say that they die in order to live, humbling themselves to find their true identity in God.

Mekomiya, Ethiopian Orthodox prayer sticks serve a dual purpose: to lean on during long prayers and as a liturgical instrument in sacred hymn and chants.

According to an Ethiopian Orthodox Monk, Emayoy Hannah Mariam, the yellow robes, hats, and wraps worn by the Ethiopian Orthodox Monks represent a life of prayer and penance. These items are reminders of their connection to the life and value of the Ethiopia's hermit Monk, Saint Tekle-Haymanote. The personal Mekomiya used by the monks for walking and leaning on during long prayers are sometimes personalized.

Overnight Trips

Overnight trips widen the possibility of traveling to some of Ethiopia's most attractive parks, breathtaking lakes, and spectacular landscapes.

Awash National Park, 211 kilometers east of Addis Ababa, is home to exotic birds, animals, and plant life. According to the Ethiopian Wildlife Conservation Authority, 462 bird species have been recorded, of which six are endemic to this area.

Opposite page: Beisa Oryx in the Awash National Park. Below: The Awash River runs through a gorge in the southern part of Awash National Park and creates spectacular waterfalls. Right: One of the many species of birds found in the park.

Wenchi Crater Lake

Wenchi Crater Lake is 155 kilometers west of Addis Ababa, between the cities of Ambo and Woliso. It is a serene, green paradise in the form of an extinct volcano. The majestic Crater Lake and the peaceful mountainous landscape are known for their panorama views.

Tiya

Tiya is a town south of Addis Ababa, known for its world heritage prehistoric burial complex (shown above). The site contains 36 stelae, including 32 carved with enigmatic symbols. Although little is known about the origin and meaning of the engraved symbols, one can contemplate the value they add as archaeological reminders of an earlier Ethiopian culture.

Adadi Mariam

Adadi Mariam (shown to the right) is a 13th century rock-hewn church 70 kilometers from Addis Ababa. Ethiopia's southernmost church of its type, it has similarities to the complex of 11 monolithic churches in Lalibela, Ethiopia.

Ankober

Ankober is a town in the central part of Ethiopia. It is known for being the capital city of the former kingdom of Shewa. This historic town was the seat of Emperor Menelik II before he moved the capital to Addis Ababa in 1886. The Ankober Palace Lodge's royal accommodations and commanding view are perfect venues to experience history while enjoying panoramic views of the surroundings.

Ankober Palace Lodge (shown above), located atop the Ankober Hills behind an extant original partial palace enclosure wall. Sides: The profiles of Emperor Menelik II and his wife, Empress Taitu, as carved on the door panels inside the main hall.

Opposite Page: An escarpment named Emperor Menelik's Window is located near the town of Debre Sina. Visitors who dare to get close enough for a good look are thrilled watching endemic gelada baboons and goats feeding on the hillside.

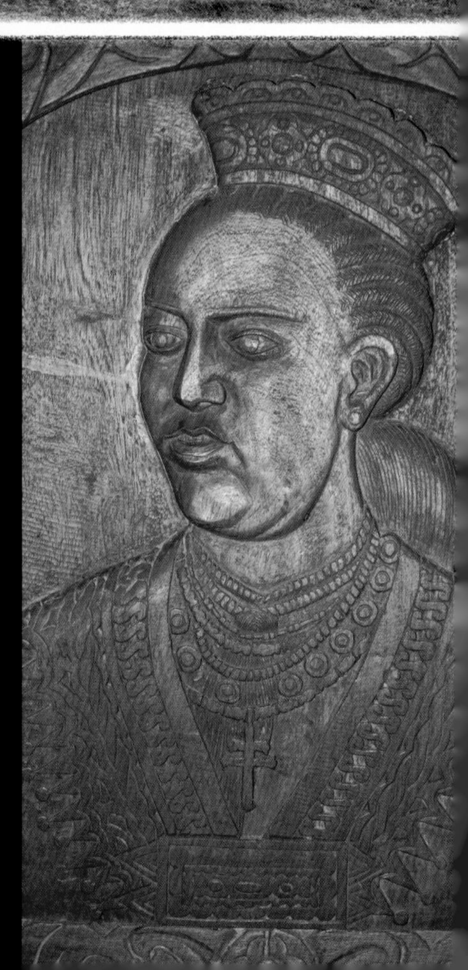

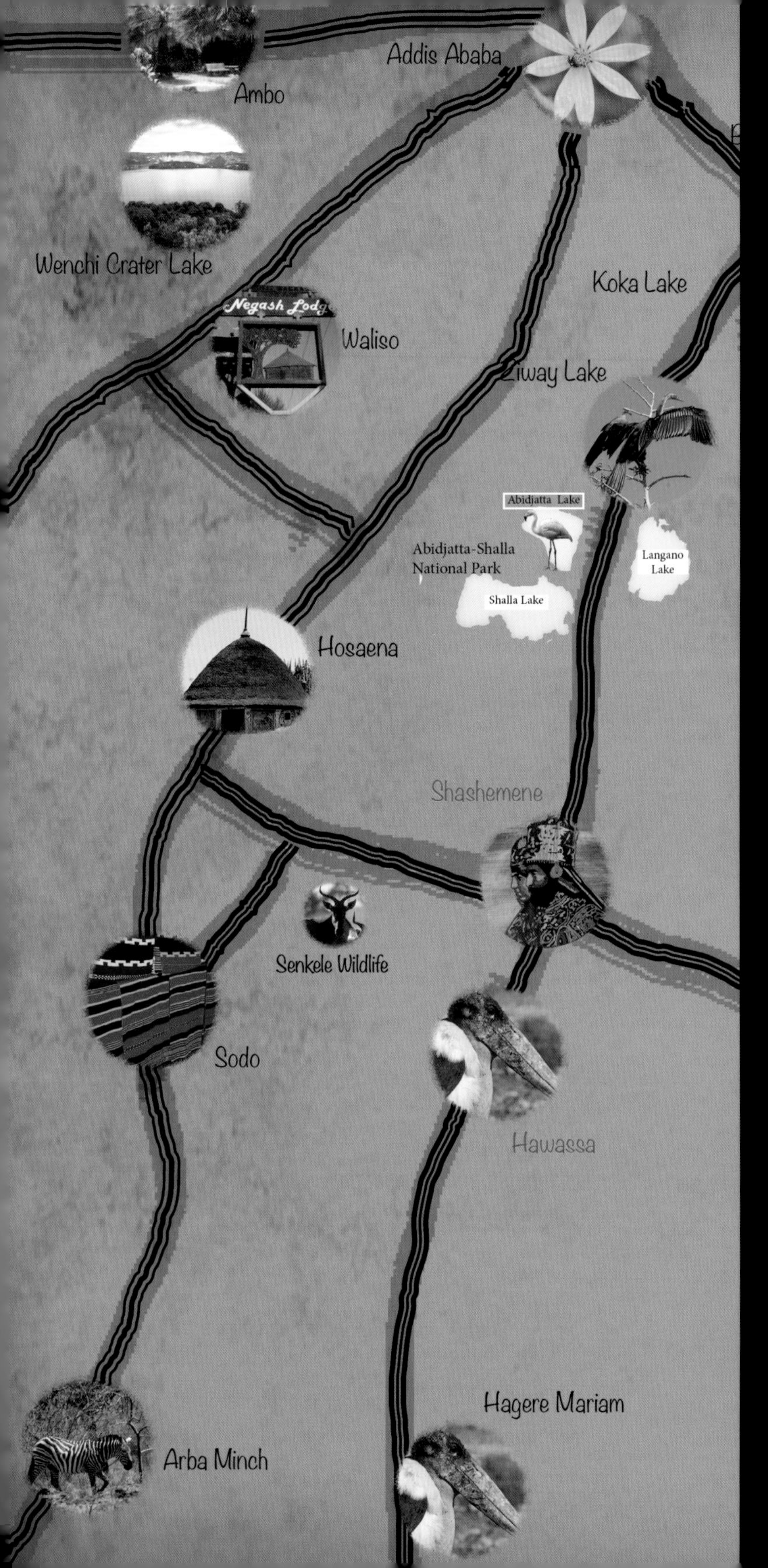

Shashemene

Shashamane is a town located 250 kilometers south of Addis Ababa. It is an important transportation hub that connects several towns in all four directions. Its southern path leads to the beautiful town of Hawassa, to Yabelo Wildlife Sanctuary and to the Kenyan border.

Shashamane is well known for its Rastafarian population. In 1948, Emperor Haile Selassie I donated 500 acres of Shashemene land to allow the settlers from Jamaica and other parts of the Caribbean to come to Africa. Today, most visitors passing by the town stop by to visit the Rastafarian communities.

HAWASSA

Hawassa is a city 270 kilometers south of Addis Ababa. The city is located near Lake Hawassa, making it a perfect place to unwind, refresh, and recharge. As the capital of the Southern Nations, Nationalities, and Peoples' Region, it is also large and modern when compared with many towns around it. Amora Gedel Park at the shore of Lake Hawassa is known for its dynamic fish market, friendly black-and-white colobus monkeys and photogenic marabou storks.

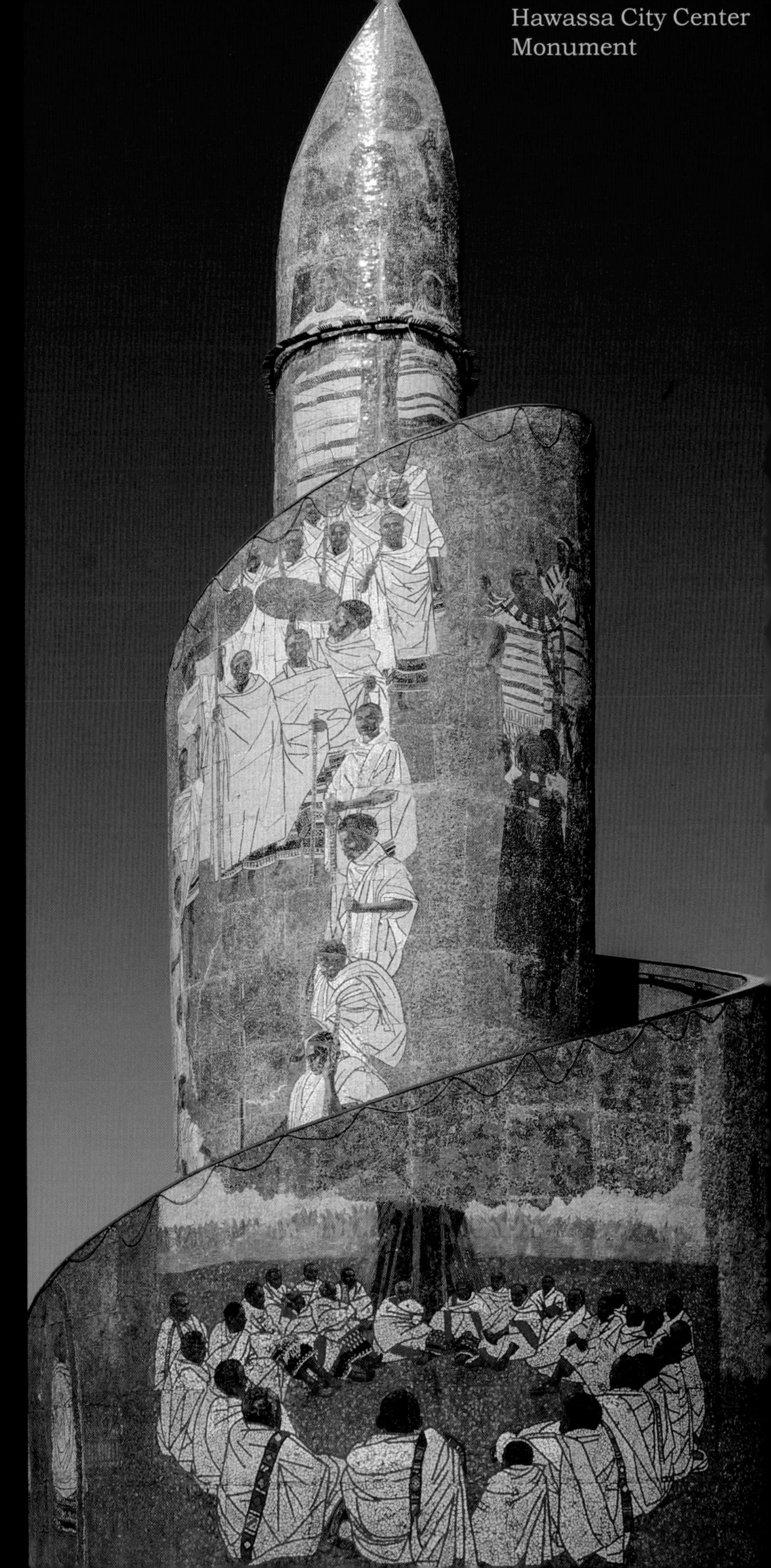

Hawassa City Center Monument

ABIJATA SHALLA NATIONAL PARK

Abijata and Shalla are alkaline lakes situated in the central section of the Ethiopian Great Rift Valley. They are part of the Abijata- Shalla National Park, located 215 kilometers south of Addis Ababa. The park covers 887 square kilometers, of which the lakes cover more than half. While Lake Abijata is shallow, Lake Shalla is the deepest lake in the Great Rift Valley, with a maximum depth measured at 260 meters. The Park was created for the many aquatic bird species that use the lakes, especially the great white pelicans.

Above: A female ostrich is looking after her chicks at the Langano ostrich farm located in the fenced-in portion of the park near the main gate. Below: Grant's gazelles are often found in small herds in the acacia woodland before reaching the lakes. Right: Flamingos feeding on the shores of the Abijata and Shalla alkaline lakes.

The main attractions of the Abijata-Shalla National Park are the number of hot springs and the large number of flamingos on the Abijata and Shalla lakes.

EXCURSIONS

Some of the most captivating scenes in Ethiopia are the result of the glowing sunsets over magnificent land formations. Excursions to all corners of the country open up opportunities to see art created when the sun descends below the horizon.

The Awash River is 225 kilometers east of Addis Ababa. Although the majestic water is as captivating to experience in daytime, it is more remarkable at sunset. A front row seat to witness nature's performance will be most rewarding when darkness overpowers and the sun becomes emotional and friendly, waving goodbye with its last rays.

Traveling to eastern Ethiopia is a voyage of the senses, emotions, and spirit of adventure. The journey includes delving into depths of curiosity to appreciate such unique activities as feeding wild animals, and yet it brings one back to the real world with natural bliss. The Awash National Park and Babile Elephant Sanctuary raise the sense of reverence, while the cities of Adama, Asebe Teferi, Harar, and Dire Dawa offer their chapters in the story we call Ethiopia.

The nightly performance of feeding hyenas is distinctive to the city of Harar. Tewodros, one of the hyena feeding experts, starts by uttering words to summon the unpredictable wild animals. As the reluctant hyenas gather to start the show, spectators are told to stand in a small and dusty area lit by vehicle headlights. Children assist Tewodros by brining sacks full of meat rejected by local butchers.

The first reactions of sheer disbelief and amazement quickly give way to a desire to participate. Initially, a piece of meat looped around the end of a long stick is used to feed the hyenas. As the comfort level of the participant increases, the length of the stick is shortened for a closer and more intense experience. The above picture shows me cautiously feeding a hyena.

Arthur Rimbaud was a French poet who became a merchant in Harar. The Rimbaud house located in Jegol, the walled city of Harar, is currently used as a center and museum for his works, letters, and publications. The dated pictures hanging on the first-floor illustrate the city's transformation.

In the rooms adjacent to the Rimbaud house, local women make premium polychrome baskets. The baskets vary in detail, type, function, color, and design to fit practical needs. The most intricate designs take days to make and are priced accordingly.

Popular Destinations East of Addis Ababa

In the town of Babille, located on the main road between Harar and Jijiga, there is an area called the Dakhata Valley. The valley is scattered with intriguing rock formation that can be seen from the main road. The area is also known for its hot springs, mineral water, and an elephant sanctuary. Below: Eastern Ethiopia offers a chance to see herd camels, perfect companions to the locals' way of life.

The Bale Mountain Park

Bale Mountains National Park (BMNP) is located 400 kilometers southeast of Addis Ababa. The Park encompasses an area of 2,200 square kilometers and comprises five major zones: Northern Grasslands, Juniper Woodland, Afroalpine Meadows, Harenna Forest, and Erica Belt.

The mountain is known for its natural trekking charm, scenic drives, and rewarding wildlife viewing experience. It is also home to many animals including endemic nyala, Ethiopian wolf, warthog, Menelik's bushbuck, and numerous species of birds.

Ethiopian endemic red fox (key kebero) at Sanetti Plateau of Bale Mountains National Park.

Bale Mountains National Park is home to over 300 species of birds, including Rougetius rougetii, the spot-breasted lapwing, the Abyssinian longclaw, the wattled crane, and the Eastern Imperial Eagle (bird of prey shown above).

Above: A mountain nyala is an attractively marked antelope found in Bale Mountains National Park. Below: A Bale Mountains warthog intuitively entering into a protective mode.

Above: Giant lobelias (known locally as jibara) are one of the plants that overcome extreme temperatures and wind to survive at Bal Mountains at an altitude which ranges from 3,100 to 4,377 meters. Below: The Sof Omar, spectacular underground caverns, ar ound in the small town of Sof Omar, about 120 kilometers from the town of Goba, Bale. The caverns are also an important Islami shrine.

BAHIR DAR

Bahir Dar is located 565 kilometers northwestern of Addis Ababa. The city is a launching pad for many of the area's tourist attractions. It presents such activities as a boat trip on Lake Tana, a drive to the Blue Nile Falls, a visit to medieval monasteries, cultural shows, or simple relaxation watching pelicans around the lake to positively influence any mood.

Right: A priest shows an ancient illustrated manuscript, Debre Maryam Monastery, Lake Tana.

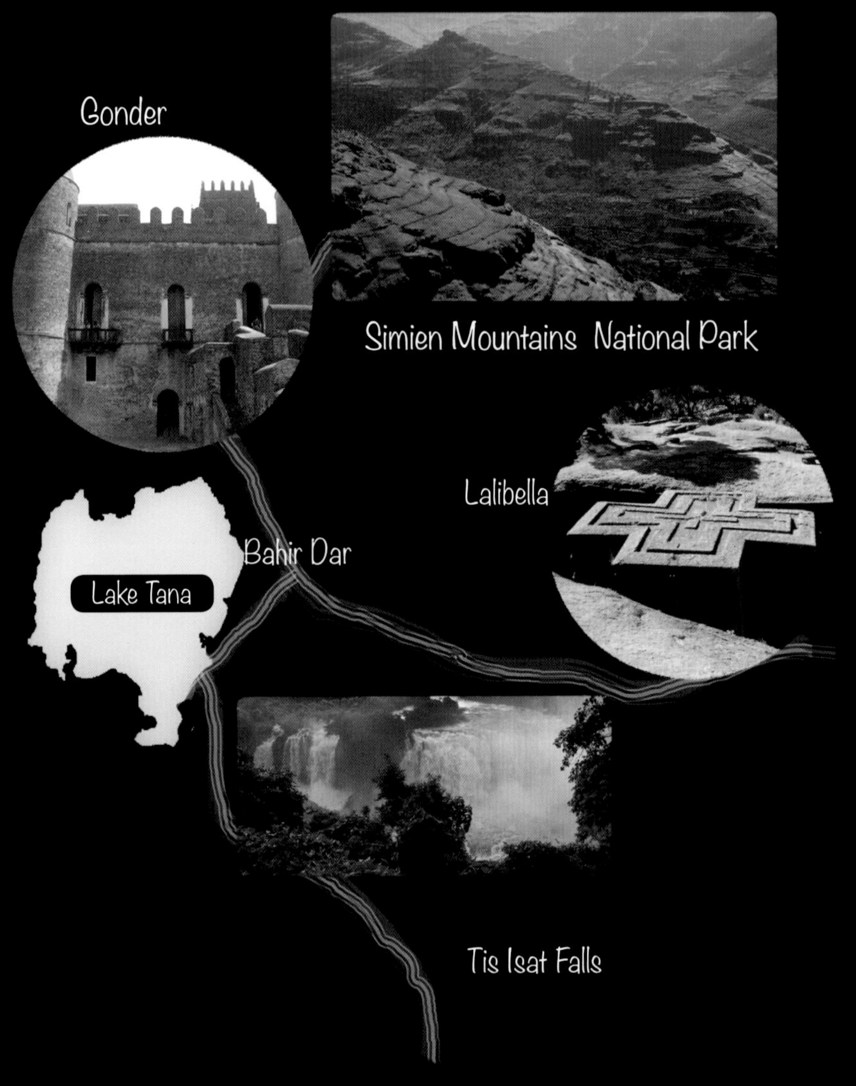

Popular Destinations in the Amhara Region

The House of Azmari (azmari bet) is where people go to listen and enjoy traditional music, often perfected by a homemade wine called tej or local beer. The word azmari refers to a masinko (a single-stringed, bowed lute) virtuoso who also sings or works with an accompanying singer. The azmaris are known for drawing from their personal experiences, current events, and unique perspectives to deliver impromptu musical humor. The experience is like getting entertained by both a skilled musician and a comedian at once. Balageru Cultural Club in Bahir Dar is shown above.

Top left: Although the Tis Isat (Blue Nile) Falls, shown above, is not at its full capacity, the absolute power illustrated by the overall scene is impressive. Top right: A small museum in the compounds of the Entos Eyesu Monastery is filled with ancient manuscripts, paintings, and artifacts from Ethiopia's early kings and queens. Below: Picturesque by day and dazzling by dusk, Lake Tana is a perfect spot to observe birds flying feverishly to get back to their nests to roost.

Lalibela

Lalibela is a city located 600 kilometers north of Addis Ababa. The city is synonymous with its monolithic churches dating back to the 12th century, and filled with mystery and beauty. Entering the rock-hewn churches educes somber appreciation of the skill and resolve required to excavate with such precision.

Lalibela's intricate church designs include equally fascinating secret tunnels, small bridges, and underground passages.

Above: One of the many ancient, hand-illustrated manuscripts found inside the 12th-century rock-hewn churches of Lalibela. Opposite Page: Saint George, one of the 11 rock-hewn churches in Lalibela.

Ne-Akute Le-Abe is a church built under a natural cave. It is located a short distance from the city of Lalibela. The church's notable dripping holy water is collected into rock pots before it is distributed to followers.

GONDER

Situated in the foothills of the Simien Mountains, the city of Gonder has earned the epithet "Camelot of Africa." The city was King Fasilides's chosen capital from 1635 to 1667. The Royal Enclosure, located near the center of the city, houses impressive castles.

A trip to Gonder is a must to witness a prime example of power, authority, and majesty. Visitors will also appreciate the 17th century murals decorating Debre Birhan Selassie Church (shown on the right).

The Royal Enclosure of Gonder, also known as Fasil Gebbi, is home to the complex of buildings founded in the 17th century. The buildings included in the compound are Fasilides's Castle (shown on the opposite page left), and the castles of Iyasu and Empress Mentewab.

Situated about five kilometers north of the city of Gonder is the Falasha village of Wolleka. Once home to Ethiopian Jews, the area is filled with articles of traditional Ethiopian Judaism.

Simien Mountains National Park

Simien Mountains National Park is located 800 kilometers northwest of Addis Ababa, near the city of Gonder. The 412-square-kilometer park was established in 1969 to protect the land and wildlife in it. The park is home to Mount Ras Dashen, the tallest peak in Ethiopia, standing 4,543 feet high.

The Park is also home to some extremely rare animals, such as the gelada baboon (also known as the bleeding-heart baboon) and the walia ibex, a goat-like animal found nowhere else in the world.

A yawning gelada baboon (also known as the bleeding-heart baboon) showing its distinct bright patch of skin on its chest.

Above left: Beautiful alpine plants, including giant lobelias and red-hot pokers, add yet further glory to the immense plateau, deep valleys, and pinnacles of the Simien Mountains. Above right: A thick-billed raven in Simien Mountains National Park near Chenneck camp, located 58 kilometers from the town of Debark.

Listed as a world heritage site since 1978, Simien Mountains National Park boasts one of the most spectacular landscapes in the world. The breathtaking scenery created by contrasts of the mountain peaks, deep valleys, and sharp cliffs stimulates the spirit and moves the heart.

Above left: Children from the Simien Mountains area often entertain visitors with local tunes and give the scenery its own indigenous soundtrack. Above right: A walia ibex, a goat-like animal, in Simien Mountains National Park near Chenneck camp. The walia ibex is found nowhere else in the world.

TIGRAY

The State of Tigray shares common borders with Eritrea on the north, the State of Afar on the east, the State of Amhara on the south, and the Republic of the Sudan on the west. The state is known for its contributions to early Ethiopian civilization and thus houses many treasures of interest to tourists. The Axum obelisks or steles, the pre-Axumite Yeha's "Temple of The Moon," the Royal Bath and Palace of the Queen of Sheba, rock-hewn churches, a holy Islamic site, and the Ark of the Covenant are among the most prominent.

Debre Damo is a monastery located on a plateau about 90 kilometers northeast of the city of Axum. The founder of Debre Damo, Abuna Aregawi, was said to have been provided with a large serpent to help him make the 15-meter climb up a sheer cliff required to reach the summit. To this day, parishioners and visitors are challenged to mimic his climb with the aid of a rope.

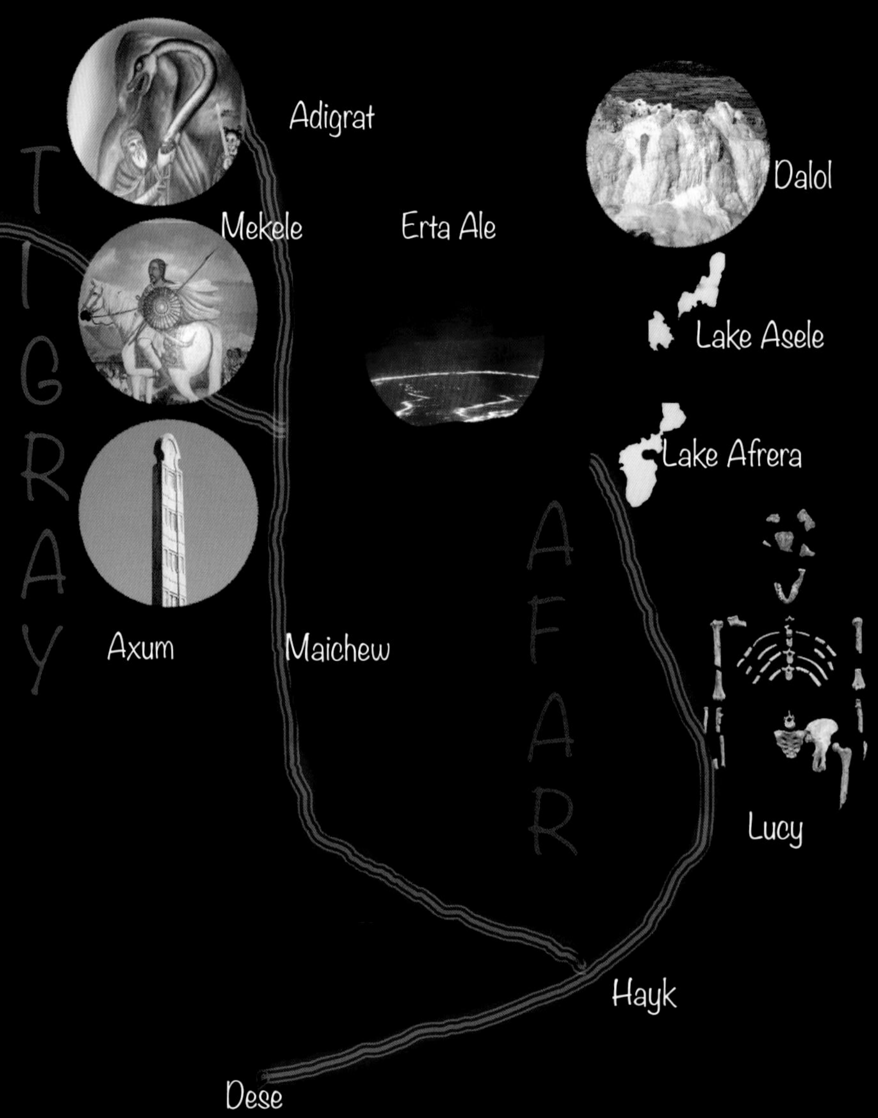

Popular Destinations in the Tigray and Afar Regions

The Tsion Maryam (Church of St. Mary of Zion) is a unique and historical location with immense importance, as it is the sanctuary for the original Ark of the Covenant. The Ark, which is said to have come to Ethiopia with Menelik I after visiting his father, King Solomon, is guarded and viewed by a single monk at the chapel, shown above. The guardian monk is appointed for life by his predecessor.

Tigray, Ethiopia's northernmost region, has more than 120 rock-hewn churches. The history and grace of the churches, simply known as the Gheralta cluster, justify the difficult climb and hike required to reach them. Abuna Yemata is one of Gheralta's rock-hewn churches. The church is carved into the cliff face of one of the mountains of Guh. Well-preserved frescoes (shown above) on the dome of the Abuna Yemata Church are among the many centuries-old works of art found there.

Negash is a village in the Tigray Region of Ethiopia about 10 kilometers north of the city of Wukro. Negash is perhaps the most important holy Islamic site for Muslims in Ethiopia, for it was the site of their first settlement in Ethiopia. Mohammed's top followers and close relatives were received in Ethiopia to escape persecution in Saudi Arabia. The new Mosque (shown above) was built in 2003 in front of a smaller Mosque that stands on the site of the 17th-century original.

Axum is a city in northern Ethiopia. Visitors to Axum will have the opportunity to see the palace of the Queen of Sheba, ancient obelisks (shown above), and the tombs of Kings Kaleb and Gebre Meskel.

Danakil Depression

The Danakil Depression is part of the Afar Triangle located in the northeastern part of Ethiopia. With the average temperature of 34–35° C, the Danakil Depression is officially the hottest place on earth. What makes the region even more compelling is that it is dotted with active volcanoes, bubbling green sulfur lakes, solidified black lava, and salt-coated landscape.

The Afar Region is also home to Erta Ale (meaning "smoking mountain" in the local Afar language), a 613-meter deep and 40-kilometer diameter base basaltic shield active volcano. Erta Ale is listed as one of the most active volcanoes in Africa.

Top: Danakil landscapes. Bottom: A camel caravan along age-old routes to the Tigray Region transports salt bars mined in the Danakil Depression. Opposite page: An impressive nighttime view of Erta Ale's active lava lake is nothing short of a carefully choreographed show. Glowing fresh lava continuously emerges from the cracks in the lake's crust before settling down to allow the next round of magma to burst out with even greater force.

South of Addis Ababa

Travelers going south of Addis Ababa should familiarize themselves with the main attractions prior to embarking on the journey. The country's most intriguing tribal cultures, fascinating landscapes, rich wildlife, and scenic lakes and parks are found in the southern region.

Popular Destinations in the South and West Regions

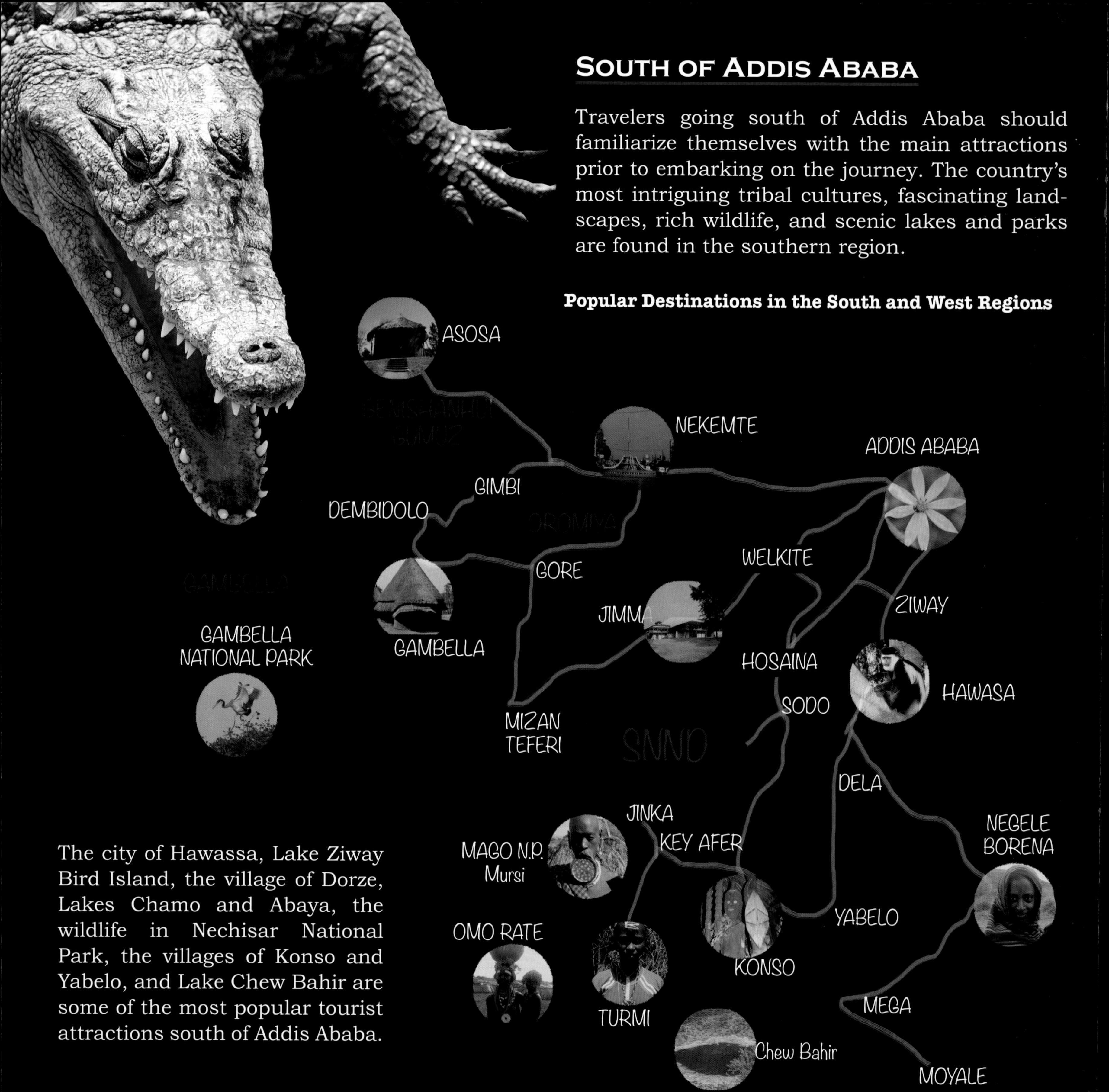

The city of Hawassa, Lake Ziway Bird Island, the village of Dorze, Lakes Chamo and Abaya, the wildlife in Nechisar National Park, the villages of Konso and Yabelo, and Lake Chew Bahir are some of the most popular tourist attractions south of Addis Ababa.

Above: Dorze homes are tall, unique structures, built with vertical hardwood poles and woven bamboo. Below: Crocodile on the shore of Lake Chamo.

Above: The natural mud towers sculpted by the occasional water flow resemble a city filled with skyscrapers. Reflecting this phenomenon, the Konso landscape is nicknamed "New York."

Above: Plains Zebras found in Nech-Sar National Park, located between Lake Abaya and Lake Chamo near the city of Arba Minch. Below: Hippopotamus in Lake Chamo

WEST OF ADDIS ABABA

The western part of Ethiopia is a rarely visited place, with untouched resources and undiscovered stories. Most visitors tend to go north for the history or south for the culture. Few are aware of the western highlands renowned for the birth of coffee, tea farming, and the country's abundant fruit production.

After leaving Addis Ababa to go west, visitors encounter various towns and cities. The town of Ambo and the Wenchie are the closest and most scenic landscapes going farther west. Nekemte, Gimbi, Gore, Mizan Teferi, and Jimma are bigger cities with their own history, character, and allure.

Above: Kefa is a predominantly highland region situated in the southwest of Ethiopia, an area commonly known for its lush green landscape and abundance of water. Just 100 meters off the main road in the Kefa Biosphere Reserve is the Woshi, a spectacular waterfall (shown above). Below: The palace of King Abba Jifar Abba Gomol of Jimma, located on the outskirts of the city in Jiren. Abba Jifar ruled over Jimma from 1878 until his death in 1933.

Above: Freshly picked coffee beans before their outer shells are removed. Below: Banana farms are common scenes in the western region of Ethiopia.

Below: Papaya is one of the major fruits growing in the western regions. Right: A woman harvesting tea leaves at one of the many tea plantations in the western region.

Coffee, Tea and Fruit

Western Ethiopia is a naturally rich area with many rolling hills and dense forests. The area is also a paradise for those looking to observe animals and bird-watching. The fertile soil is another reason that wild coffee, planted coffee, fruit trees, and vegetables are found almost everywhere in the region.

One of the groups in the lower Omo valley, the Hamer people, are known for their elaborate attire, cultural ceremonies, and unpretentious pride. A boy's coming-of-age in the Hamer tribe is measured by his successful jumping over bulls. In the ceremony, a number of bulls are lined up and restrained from the slightest movement to allow the *ukuli* (man-to-be) to make the jump. If successful, he earns *maz* status; that is, he is part of the Hamer adult society, ready to accept such responsibilities as marriage.

Before the *ukuli* is ready to jump the bulls, the youngest women of his family mark the occasion with dancing, singing, and blowing of their trumpets. The ladies also decorate their hair and body with a mixture of red clay and butter, and they wear a short skirt made of goatskin. After a successful jump, the celebration continues the next night, with yet another festival, called Evangadi.

The Lower Omo River Valley is also known for the other tribes in the area. When visiting the Valley, it is common to encounter people from such tribes as the Arbore, Ari, Bena, Bodi, Bumi, Daasanech, Hamer, Karo, Kwegu, Mursi, Tsemay, and Turkana. Most tribes are known for such practices as decorative scarring, and body piercing. The people from the Mursi tribe, for example, are renowned for their practice of wearing clay lip plates.

The Monday market at Turmi, the Saturday market at Dimek and the Thursday market at Key Afer are great places to fir locally made jewelry and other souvenirs.

Above left: Hamer ladies returning from the Dimeka market. Their hair is decorated with a mixture of red clay and butter, and they ar wearing beads decorating short goatskin skirts. Above right: Visiting the Omorate village requires crossing the Omo River in a dugou

GAMBELA

The Gambela Peoples' Region lies at the western tip of Ethiopia, bordering the Sudan on the west, south, and north; the Southern Nations, Nationalities, and Peoples' Region on the south and east; and the Oromia Region on the north and east. The Gambela Region is home to the Baro River, which is vital to the region as a source of power and transportation and for supporting fishing and farming activities.

The culture, traditional food, and home styles of the Gambela native tribes—the Anuak, Majaneger, Opo, Kumo, and Nuer—are distinct to the tribes and attractive to visitors.

bove: A Nuer tribe hut design is identified by the veranda-like ront extension. Below: A photo showing an Anuak woman smoking a water pipe in her courtyard.

Gambela National Park is home to many species of animals and birds. Among the animals found in the Park are the Nile lechwe buffalo, elephant, white-eared kob, and roan antelope.

The State of Benishangul-Gumuz is located in the western part of Ethiopia. The state shares common boundaries in the west with North and South Sudan, in the northeast with the State of Amhara, and in the east and south with the State of Oromia. The area is home to five ethnic groups: the Berta, Shinasha, Mao, Gumuz, and Komo.

The Benishangul-Gumuz Region is well known for its gold deposits, evident by the number of residents performing small-scale gold mining. The cultural museum located in its capital, Assosa, is a great place to acquire knowledge about the five tribes and the area's long connection to gold.

The region's distinguished leader, Sheikh Ojale, is known to be a champion of unity. His contributions to the development of Ethiopia and the resistance of the Italian invasion are documented through his letter exchanges with the central government of Emperor Menelik and Emperor Haile Selassie. These letters are housed in the cultural museum.

This small round hut, made out of mud and straw is located in Assosa. Sheikh Ojale is said to have used the hut as a traditional village court to resolve conflicts and hand down judgments. Below: Zumbara, a unique style of song and energetic dance from the Berta people of Benishangul-Gumuz Region.

National Parks and Wildlife Sanctuaries

Abijata Shalla Lakes National Park

Distance from Addis Ababa: 215 KM

Region: Oromia

Year Established: 1973

Area: 887 km2

Key Species: white pelican, great and lesser flamingos and African fish eagle.

Alitash National Park

Distance from Addis Ababa: 1025 KM

Region: Amhara

Year Established: 2005

Area: 2666 km2

Key Species: elephant, greater and lesser kudu, lion and leopard.

Arsi Mountain Park

Distance from Addis Ababa: 225 KM

Region: Oromia

Year Established: 2010

Area: 1200 km2

Key Species: mountain nyala, Menelik's bushbuck, Ethiopian wolf, leopard, African wild dogs,

Awash National Park

Distance from Addis Ababa: 215 KM

Region: Afar and Oromia

Year Established: 1966

Area: 756 km2

Key Species: beisa oryx, waterbuck, sommering gazelle, greater and lesser kudu and swayne's hartebeest

Bahirdar Tikur Abay Millennium Park

Distance from Addis Ababa: 560 KM

Region: Afar and Amhara

Year Established: 2008

Area: 43 km2

Key Species: hippopotamus, crocodile, various specious of birds

Bakusa Park

Distance from Addis Ababa: 715 KM

Region: Afar and Amhara

Year Established: 2012

Area: 446 km2

Key Species: greater kudu, oribi, leopard and lion

Bale Mountains National Park

Distance from Addis Ababa: 400 KM

Region: Afar and Oromia

Year Established: 1970

Area: 1250 km2

Key Species: mountain nyala, Menelik's bushbuck, Ethiopian wolf, leopard, lion, bohor reedbuck, bale monkey and Abyssinian Hare.

Borena Saynt Park

Distance from Addis Ababa: 596 KM

Region: Afar and Amhara

Year Established: 2009

Area: 44 km2

Key Species: Menelik's bushbuck, gelada baboon, Abyssinian hare, 11 endemic plant species

Chebera Churchura Park

Distance from Addis Ababa: 460 KM

Region: Southern Nations, Nationalities, and People's

Year Established: 2005

Area: 1190 km2

Key Species: elephant, hippopotamus, buffalo, lion, leopard and waterbuck

Dati Wolel Park

Distance from Addis Ababa: 750 KM

Region: Oromia

Year Established: 2006

Area: 431 km2

Key Species: hippopotamus, buffalo, lion, various species of water birds

Gambella National Park

Distance from Addis Ababa: 840 KM

Region: Gambella

Year Established: 1974

Area: 4575 km2

Key Species: nile lechwe, buffalo, elephant, white-eared kob, roan antelope, giraffe, topi/tiang and hippopotamus.

Geralle National Park

Distance from Addis Ababa: 890 KM

Region: Somali

Year Established: 2006

Area 3858 km2

Key Species: elephant, greater and lesser kudu, beisaoryx, gerenuk and ostrich

Gibe Seleko Park

Distance from Addis Ababa: 174 KM

Region: Southern Nations, Nationalities, and People's

Year Established: 2009

Area: 431 km2

Key Species: mountain nyala and lion

Kafta Shiraro National Park

Distance from Addis Ababa: 1015 KM

Region: Tigray

Year Established: 2007

Area: 2117 km2

Key Species: greater kudu, elephant and roan antelope

Lake Abaya Park

Distance from Addis Ababa: 352 KM

Region: Southern Nations, Nationalities, and People's

Year Established: 2009

Area: 248 km2

Key Species: wild dogs, buffalo and line

Mago National Park

Distance from Addis Ababa: 460 KM

Region: Southern Nations, Nationalities, and People's

Year Established: 1979

Area: 1942 km2

Key Species: elephant, buffalo and lesser kudu

Maze Park

Distance from Addis Ababa: 460 KM

Region: Southern Nations, Nationalities, and People's

Year Established: 2005

Area: 202 km2

Key Species: swiyne's hartebeest, oribi

Nech-Sar National Park

Distance from Addis Ababa: 502 KM

Region: Southern Nations, Nationalities, and People's

Year Established: 1974

Area: 514 km2

Key Species: burchell's zebra, greater and lesser kudu, swayne's hartebeest, borena gazelle, crocodile and African wild dog.

Omo National Park

Distance from Addis Ababa: 867 KM

Region: Southern Nations, Nationalities, and People's

Year Established: 1967

Area: 4065 km2

Key Species: common eland, buffalo, elephant, cheetah,lion,giraffe, and African wild dog.

Simien Mountains National Park

Distance from Addis Ababa: 800 KM

Region : Amhara

Year Established: 1967

Area: 412 km2

Key Species: walia ibex, Ethiopian wolf, gelada monkey and klipspringer

Yangudi Rasa National Park

Distance from Addis Ababa: 430 KM

Region: Afar

Year Established: 1977

Area: 4731 km2

Key Species: wild Ass, sommerin and dorcas gazelle, ostrich and grevy's zebra.

Babile Elephant Sanctuary

Distance from Addis Ababa: 557 KM

Region: Somali and Oromia

Year Established: 1970

Area: 6987 km2

Key Species: elephant, lion and lesser kudu.

Senkele Swayne's Hartebeest Sanctuary

Distance from Addis Ababa: 300 KM

Region: Oromia and Southern Nations, Nationalities, and People's

Year Established: 1974

Area: 54 km2

Key Species: swayne's hartebeest, bohor reedbuck, oribi, leopard, greater kudu.

Yabello Wildlife Sanctuary

Distance from Addis Ababa: 570 KM

Region: Oromia

Year Established: 1986

Area: 2500 km2

Key Species: burchell's zebra, ostrich, borena gazelle.

Menze Guassa Community Conservation

Distance from Addis Ababa: 260 KM

Region: Amhara

Year Established: 2012

Area: 100 km2

Key Species: gelada baboon, Ethiopian wolf, birds or prey

Culture and Tourism Bureaus

Post Office Box 8663 Addis Ababa, Ethiopia
Tel. +251 11 859 11 44/+251-11-552-7188
Fax 251-11-552-7181
E-mail: info@addisculturetourism.gov.et/
Web: www.addisculturetourism.gov.et/

Dire Dawa Administration Council Tourism
Development and Promotion Core Process
Tel. +251 25 111 5657
Fax +251 25 111 1072/+251 25 111 5454

Tigray National Regional Government
Culture and Tourism Agency
Post Office Box 124, Mekelle, Ethiopia
Tel. +251 34 440 1031
Fax +251 34 440 1032
Email: Tigrai.tourisum@ethionet.net

Amhara National Regional Government
Culture and Tourism
Post Office Box 1616 Nahir Dar, Ethiopia
Tel. +251 58 220 1132
Fax +251 58 220 2650
Email: Amhtour@ethionet.et
www.amharatourisum.org.et/tourism

Afar National Regional Government Culture and Tourism
Post Office Box 46, Semera, Ethiopia
Tel. +251 33 666 0488
Fax +251 33 666 0209

Oromia National Regional Government Culture and Tourism Agency
Post Office Box 30061, Addis Ababa, Ethiopia
Tel. +251 11 554 1702/01
+251 11 554 1713/01
Fax +251 11 554 9464
Email: Oromiactb@ethionet.et

Somali National Regional Government Culture and Tourism Agency, Jigjiga
Post Office Box 365, Jigjiga, Ethiopia
Tel. +251 25 775 3027

Harari People National Regional
Government Culture and Tourism Agency
Post Office Box 123 (581), Harar, Ethiopia
Tel. +251 25 666 1961
Fax +251 25 666 9090

Benshangul Gumez National Regional Government Culture and Tourism, Asossa
Tel. +251 57 775 1264
+251 57 775 1267
Fax +251 11 775 0845

Gambella People Gumez National Regional Government Culture and Tourism
Tel. +251 47 551 2925
+251 47 551 2351
Fax +251 11 775 0845

South N/N/P/N National Regional Government Culture and Tourism Bureau, Hawassa
Post Office Box 1078, Hawassa, Ethiopia
Tel. +251 46 220 8490
+251 46 220 5887
Fax +251 58 220 5197
Email: bureau@southtourism.gove.et
Web: www.southtourisum.gov.et

would like to express my gratitude to the many people who saw me through this book. My thanks to all those who provided support, talked things over, read, wrote, offered comments, allowed me to quote their remarks and assisted in the editing, proofreading and design.

Alehubel Teshome ▪ Alemayehu Fanta ▪ Alula Kebede ▪ Amare Kibebew ▪ Berhanu Ashagrie ▪ Dagemawi Sisay ▪ Derese Demese ▪ Desalegn Mekonnen ▪ Emahoy Hannah Mariam ▪ Ephrem Gino ▪ Ezra Abate ▪ Feleke Hailu ▪ Fentahun Tiruneh, ▪ Fiseha Damta ▪ Getachew Debalke ▪ Kalkidan Addis ▪ Kebede Balcha ▪ Kibret Zekiwos ▪ Marie Claire Andrea ▪ Matt Andrea ▪ Melaku Belay ▪ Minasse Wondimu ▪ Myrna McCullin Smith ▪ Senedu Araya-Sellassie ▪ Solome Asseres ▪ Tadesse Belaineh Habtemariam ▪ Tekleyohannes Zike ▪ Tewodros “Teddy” Tefera ▪ Tigestu Tadesse ▪ Webshet Abebaw - Chapy Ethiopia ▪ Yemane Zemenfeskidus ▪ Yohannes Afework ▪ Zelaelem Tefera ▪ Zinash Tsegay

I wish to thank the following institutions for their contributions to my inspiration and knowledge in creating this book:

Abshirokids ▪ Addis Ababa Football Federation ▪ Addis Ababa Culture and Tourism Bureau ▪ Addis Ababa University Yared School of Music ▪ Addis Ababa University Alle School of Fine Arts and Design ▪ Born Free Ensessakotteh ▪ Chane Restaurant ▪ Cupcake Delights Bakery ▪ Ethiopian Airlines ▪ Ethiopian Culture and Tourism Bureau ▪ Ethiopian Embassy in Washington DC ▪ Ethiopian Mapping Agency ▪ Ethiopian Foreign Minister ▪ Ethiopian Twice Boutique ▪ Fendika Cultural Club ▪ Four Start Band ▪ Guramayle Art Center ▪ Hager Fikir Theater ▪ Makush Art Gallery ▪ Mini Ethiopia Exhibits ▪ National Theater ▪ Patriarchate Museum ▪ K-Design Rahel Zewda ▪ Saint George Cathedral ▪ Saint George Art Gallery ▪ Sheraton Addis ▪ Taka Negest Beata Lemariam Church ▪ Taitu Hotel ▪ U.S. Library of Congress.

Photo Credits

Addis Ababa Culture and Tourism Bureau: Page 7 - Addis Ababa at its formation. Page 19 – Legehar Terminal at its formation. Page 76 - One of the first cars in Addis Ababa. Page 79 – Gotterra Interchange. Page 83 – Eid al-Fitr Festival

Minasse Wondimu: Page 8 and 107–AU Rotunda. Page 75 - The Great Ethiopian Run Page 77 – Train, Addis Ababa Light Rail Project. Page 83 - Anwar Mosque. Page 84 – Festival

Kebede Balcha: Page 12 - Emperor Menelik II. Page 15 – National Palace and Emperor Haile Selassie.

Getachew Tekeste Wessena: Ethiopian Football Federation: - Page 75 - The Ethiopian National Football Team at a qualifier game in Addis Ababa. & Diehard fans wearing the national team's jersey. **Asrar Lulseged:** Page 117, Langano

John Rizzo: Page 155, Freshly Picked coffee. **Kalkidan Addis:** Page 142 - Blue Nile Falls.

Further Resources

Addis Ababa Cultural & Tourism Bureau. *Exploration Guide For Addis Ababa City & The Surrounding Areas.* Camerapix, 2009.

Adejumobi, Saheed A. *The History of Ethiopia: The Greenwood Histories of the Modern Nations*: Greenwood Press, 2007.

African Bird Club. *Working for birds in Africa, Bale Mountain National Park, Ethiopia* (2012), Retrieved from http://www.africanbirdclub.org/content/bale-mountain-national-park-ethiopia

Aklilu, Amsalue. A *glimpse on Ethiopia.* The Public Relations Department MIDROCK Ethiopia, 1999

Amin, Mohamed, Duncan Willetts. *Ethiopian: A Tourist Paradise.* Ethiopian Tourism Commission: Camerapix, 1996

Amin, Mohamed, Duncan Willetts & Alastair Matheson. *Journey Through ETHIOPIA.* Ethiopian Tourism Commission, Camerapix, 1997

Asrat, Asfawossen, Metasebia Demisse & Aberra Mogessie. *Geotourism in Ethiopia.* Shama Books, Addis Ababa, Ethiopia, 2008.

Badejo, L. Badejo. *Ethiopia: The African Union.* Infobase Publishing, 2008

Batistoni, Milena and Gian Paolo Chiari. *The Old Tracks in the New Flower: A historical Guide to Addis Ababa.* Arada Books, Addis Ababa, 2004.

Birds of the Bale Mountains National Park. (n.d.) Retrieved from http://balemountains.org/wildlife/birds/

Buxton, Davis. *Travels in Ethiopia.* Gale & Polden Limited, 1949/1951

Corona, Laurel. *Modern Nations of The World: ETHIOPIA.* Lucent Books, Inc, San Diego, CA, USA, 2001.

Ethio Telecom. *Ethiopia: National Phone Book Directory.* 2014.

Ethiopian wildlife conservation Authority (EWCA). *Parks and Sanctuaries.* (n.d.) Retrieved from http://www.ewca.gov.et/en/national_parks_and_sanctuaries_in_ethiopia

Feseha, Mulugeta. *Participatory Tourism: The Future of Ethiopia: Community Based Ecotourism Development from research to implementation. Model from Adwa, Northern Ethiopia.* Eclipse PLS, Addis Ababa, Ethiopia, 2010.

Fetahe, Rufael. *His Holiness Abune Paulos, International Figure.* EOTC, 2000.

Fradin, Dennis Brindell. *ETHIOPIA: Enchantment of the World.* Regensteiner Publication Enterprise, Inc: 1988

Gish, Steven, Winnie Thay and Zawiah Abdul Latif. *Cultures of the World: Ethiopia.* Marshall Cavendish Benchmark, Tarrytown, NY, 2006.

Gobezie, Mengistu. *Lalibela: A Museum of Living Rocks.* Gibezie Mengistu, Addis Ababa, 2012.

Gzalbez, Javier and Dulce Cebrian, Touching Ethiopia, Shama Books, Addis Ababa 2002.

Harrassowitz, Verlag Wiesbaden: Encyclopaedia Aethiopica:

Encyclopaedia Aethiopica III,Siegbert Uhlig (ed.), Harrassowitz Verlag:Wiesbaden, 2007, 541-542

Hailemelekot, Abebe. *The Victory of Adowa: The 1st Victory of Africa Over Colonialists: Commercial Printing Enterprise, Addis Ababa, Ethiopia.* 1998.

Haile Mariam, Mitiku and Abate Haile. A *Pocket Guide to Southern Nationals Nationalities and People Region.* The Southern Nations, Nationalities and Peoples Region Culture, Information and Tourism Bureau, June 1999.

Hancock, Graham. *The Beauty of ADDIS ABABA.* Camerapix Publications International, Nairobi, Kenya. 1995.

Hancock, Graham, Richard Pankhurst & Duncan Willetts. *Under the Ethiopian Skies*, editions HL, Nairobi, Kenya, 1983.

Heinrichhs, Ann. *Ethiopia: Enchantment of the World.* Children Press, 2005

Henry, Emma & Isabel Blair. *The River Of Life In Ethiopia.* 1952

Imperial Ethiopian Government Ministry of P.T. & T. (n.d.), Ethiopian Stamp Catalogue, Jirga Ltd

Lye, Keith: *Take a Trip to Ethiopia.* Franklin Watts Limited, 1986

Merahi, Kefyalew. *The contribution of the Orthodox Tewahedo Church to the Ethiopian Civilization.* Commercial Printing Enterprise, Addis Ababa, Ethiopia, 1999.

Merahi, Kefyalew. *Christianity in Ethiopia II*: Commercial Printing Enterprise, Addis Ababa, Ethiopia, 2009.

Merahi, Kefyalew. *The Most Versatile Ethiopian Scholar, St. Yared and His Outstanding Works.* Kessis Kefyalew Merahi, Addis Ababa, Ethiopia, 2004.

Mekele Tourism Retrieved form http://www.mekellecity.com/tourism.asp?site=Gheralta

Nomachi, Kazuyoshi. *Bless Ethiopia.* Odyssey Publications Limited and Pacific Press Service Limited, Tokyo, 1998.

Pankhurst, Richard. *The Ethiopians: A History The People Of Africa.* Blackwell Publication, Main Street, Malden, MA, 1998, 2001.

Pankhurst, Richard & Denis Gerard. *Ethiopia Photographed, Historic photographs of the Country and Its People Taken between 1867 and 1935.* Koutledge, 2013.

Phillips, Briggs. *Ethiopia: Highlights.* Bradt Travel Guide Ltd

Phillips, Matt, Jean-Bernard Carillet. *Ethiopia & Eritrea.* Lonely Planet, 2006

Prouty, Chris. *Empress Taytu and Menilek II: Ethioopia 1883-1910.* The Read Sea Press, Trenton, New Jersey, 1986

Rampone, Oscar. *A Souvenir Book on A Journey in ETHIOPIA.* Modena, Italy 1973

Richman, Eliza and Biniyam Admassu. *Bale Mountains National Park: A TRAVELLER'S GUIDEBOOK (2013).* Frankfurt Zoological Society and the Bale Mountains National Retrieved form http://balemountains.org/wp-content/uploads/2013/11/bale-travel-guidebook-web.pdf Tracks in the new Flower

Schemenauer, Elma. *Faces and Places: Ethiopia.* The Child World, inc. , USA, 2001

Sisay, Ayalew, Gitim Beksa and Estifanos Admasu. *A Guide to Addis Ababa.* MCBS, Ethiopia

Sisay, Ayalew. *Historical Development of Travel and Tourism in Ethiopia.* Dr. Ayalew Sisay, Addis Ababa, Ethiopia, 2009.

Sheen, Barbara: *Foods of Ethiopia.* Gale Cengage Learning, Addis Ababa, Ethiopia, 2008.

Tadesse, Bantalem. *A Guide To The Intangible Treasures of Ethiopia: Historic Perspective and Symbolic Interpretations of Festivals.* Bantalem Tadesse, 2010

Tadesse, Kebede: *Trees of Ethiopia: A photographic Guide and Description.* Washera Publishers, Addis Ababa, Ethiopia, 2012

United Nations Organization for Education, Science and Culture (UNESCO). *World Heritage List* (n.d.), Retrieved form http://whc.unesco.org/en/list

United Nations Economic Commission for Africa. *Overview.* (n.d.) Retrieved from http://www.uneca.org/pages/overview

Wenchi Eco-Tourism Association (WETA). *The Place.* (n.d.) Retrieved from http://www.wenchi-crater-lake.com/place.php

Zakari, Ahmed, Bahru Zewde, Taddese Beyene. *Proceeding of the International Symposium of the Century of Addis Ababa.* Commercial Printing Enterprise, Addis Ababa, Ethiopia, 1987.

KERANYO
ABENET
AMESTGNA
TOR HAYLOCH
LIDETA
MEXICO
OLD AIRPORT
TEMENJA YAZI
WEYRA SEFER
SARBET
MEKANISA
Aba Jifar
Gedam Iyesus
EIAGC
WO 02
Great Reformation Int.
Keranyo Medhane Alem
Geja Kale Hiwot
WO 04
WO 03
Gymnasium
Abenet
Burundi Str.
WO 08
Lideta Mekane Iyesus
Dejazmach Balcha Aba Nefso Str.
Dejazmach Bekele Weya Str.
Sao Tome and Principe Str.
Dejazmach Welde Mikael Str.
Liberiya Str.
NMA
Hotel Di Afrique
Wabi Shebele
Armed Referal And Teaching
FHC
Chad Str.
De.J.Balcha
ERCS
Police
ECX
MOCT
FPHO
Mahdere Sebhat Lideta Maryam
Medhane Alem
ESD
WO 01
WO 10
Mexico Sq.
Mulu Wengel
WO 09
Smuts Str.
MOD
Tsion Kidist Maryam Monastry
Fistula
Union Apartement
Addis Ababa Golf Club
Kolfe Keranyo
Umma
Muti Kidus Giyorgis
Cardia
Tikur A
NM
RF
Lideta
MOCT
MOH
Sudan
FCA
ESTE
EWLCA
TCD
EEPC
EPE
ERED
MOFA
Ras Lulseged Str.
Roosevelt Str.
EPSC
Genet
ETE
Ethiopian Kale Hiwot
WO 11
AU
Mozambique Str.
Mauritania Str.
Fitawrari Damtew Str.
Hotel Di France
King's
International Evangelical
WO 06
Karl Sq.
Pushkin
Pushkin Sq.
Seychelles Str.
Kidus Mikael
Tezena
Talisman
Sost Kutir Mazoriya Sq.
Eastern
South Africa Str.
Bisrate Gebriel
Eth. Guenet
Sarbetoch Full Gospel Believers
ORB
Deber Mihiret Mikael
Libya Str.
Brook
WO 03
Dacim Millennium
Alexander Pushkin Str.
Kera Selam
Tanzania Str.
Egypt Str.
WO 04
Abadir
WO 05
Alert Sq.
Alert
WO 01
Abune Aregawi
Abimaya
Yilma
Lesetho Str.
Abo
Baptist General Conference Mission
Gedo Cave
Guinea Bissau Str.
Gota
WO 05
WO 02
Gofa Kidane Mihiret